CLEVELAND'S
Public Golf Courses

A Player's Guide

CLEVELAND'S
Public Golf Courses
A Player's Guide

John H. Tidyman

GRAY & COMPANY, PUBLISHERS
CLEVELAND

For Yoshiro Takaoka, M.D., PH.D.
A Man of Grace

Copyright © 1992 by John H. Tidyman

All rights reserved. No part of this book may be reproduced or transmitted in any form or manner without written permission from the publisher, except in the case of brief quotations embodied in critical articles and reviews.

Gray & Company, Publishers
11000 Cedar Avenue
Cleveland, Ohio 44106

Library of Congress Cataloging in Publication Data
Tidyman, John H., 1949–
Cleveland's public golf courses: a player's guide.
p. cm.
1. Golf courses—Ohio—Cleveland Metropolitan Area—Directories. I. Title.
GV983.C57T53   1992
796.352´06´80977132—DC20   92-10056

ISBN 0-9631738-0-4

FIRST PRINTING
Printed in the United States of America

10 9 8 7 6 5 4 3 2 1

X Ent. Book

Contents

Map vii
Introduction ix

The Courses:

1	Airport Greens	1
2	Astorhurst	5
3	Auburn Springs	10
4	Avondale	13
5	Berkshire Hills	17
6	Big Met	21
7	Big Springs	26
8	Black Brook	30
9	Bob-O-Link	34
10	Boston Hills	39
11	Brandywine	43
12	Briardale Greens	47
13	Briarwood	51
14	Brunswick Hills	57
15	Bunker Hill	61
16	Chardon Lakes	65
17	Cherokee Hills	69
18	Creekwood	73
19	Deer Track	77
20	Dorlon Park	81
21	Emerald Woods	84
22	Erie Shores	89
23	Fairway Pines	93
24	Forest Hills	97

25	Fowler's Mill	101
26	Gleneagles	107
27	Grantwood	111
28	Highland Park	115
29	Hilliard Lakes	121
30	Hinckley Hills	124
31	Ironwood	129
32	Lost Nation	133
33	Manakiki	137
34	Painesville	142
35	Pine Brook	147
36	Pine Hills	150
37	Pine Valley	155
38	Pleasant Hill	158
39	Pleasant Valley	162
40	Pleasant View	165
41	Punderson State Park	168
42	Ridge Top	172
43	Ridgewood	176
44	Riverside	180
45	Royal Crest	185
46	Seneca	188
47	Shawnee Hills	193
48	Skyland	196
49	Sleepy Hollow	200
50	Springvale	205
51	Sweetbriar	208
52	Tam O'Shanter	212
53	Thunder Hill	217
54	Valleaire	222
55	Western Reserve	225
56	Willow Creek	229
57	Windmill Lakes	233

Contents vii

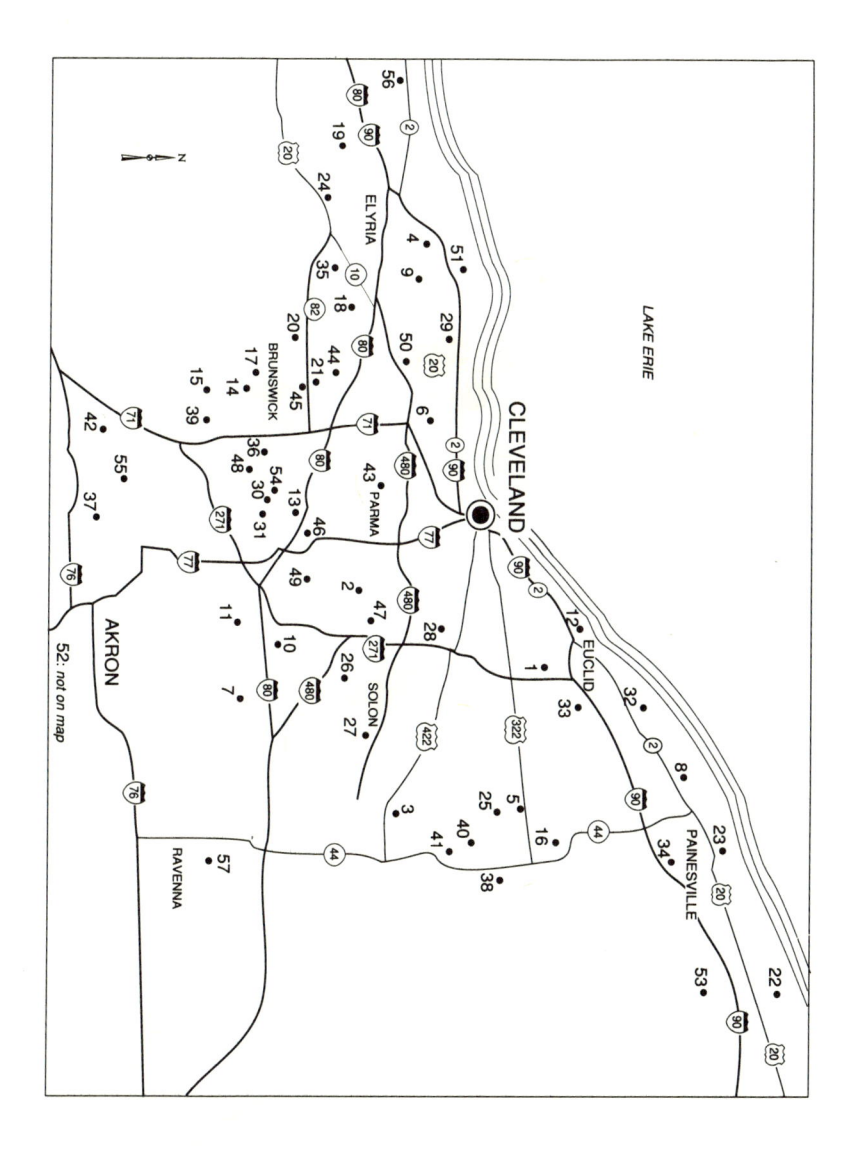

A Note on Method

The author researched this book by playing the courses and interviewing owners, managers, and customers. He collected both hard data and anecdote. His intent was to distill the virtues of each course into an entertaining, accurate description. These, it is hoped, can be used by players to savor and select among the great number and wide variety of golf courses available in this area.

Courses were chosen for inclusion based on simple criteria: they must be open to the public; they must be full-length and include 18 holes or more; they must be located within an easy drive of downtown and thus accessible to most Clevelanders.

Each chapter covers a single golf course and includes background information, a descriptive overview of the layout, and specific course data. Descriptive text was compiled from the author's first-hand research. Data were collected principally from management responses to a formal survey and from course literature. While a concerted effort was made to collect accurate data, such information is, of course, subject to change. Readers may wish to call ahead to verify prices, times, etcetera.

Prices are listed as for: 9 holes / 18 holes. Where accurate prices were not available for the coming season, last year's were listed (and noted) for use in comparison. Any data that were unobtainable were listed as "n/a"—not available, or "n/r"—not rated.

The author continues his research and welcomes comments and suggestions for future editions; he can be reached by mail in care of the publisher.

Introduction

Golf. It draws to its dimpled breast the brave, the strong, and the courageous. Somebody, after all, has to own and operate the courses.

For players, it gathers in the doughty and the desperate, the towering successes and the abject failures. It does not care about race, nationality, income, criminal records, sex, age, marital status, religious persuasion, height, weight, or color of eyes. To righties and lefties, to the bald and the hirsute, to Tories and Whigs, it offers the greatest gift: Hope.

Every time we address the ball, we believe we are going to strike it properly. And properly striking a golf ball, whether repeatedly or once every ten swings, is the purest form of delight.

Luckily, we live in a region that offers plenty of opportunity to pursue this delight. We have golf courses in quantity, and in quality, too. The game is played here in valleys, on plains, and over hills—golfing terrain that was created when the glaciers slid across North America, scooping out water hazards such as the Great Lakes.

This book was researched and written to expose the incredible wealth of public courses that makes Greater Cleveland an unheralded golf paradise. Over 1,200 holes were studied, at 57 courses—each easily accessible, thanks to the interstate highway system. Owners, pros, greenskeepers, and players were interviewed. Golf stories—evidence that the game is an addiction—were collected and are shared here with likeminded men and women.

There is no instruction between the covers. That's for the professionals. What is presented here is an armchair tour; a smorgasbord of golf. Players familiar with courses will compare notes and perhaps take issue with the author. Those unfamiliar will learn a great deal about nearby courses and likely plan to sample the feast.

This guide sought neither advertising nor sponsorship. No editorial restraints were put on the author. Still, it is a bit subjective. The author, after all, has yet to break 80. (His best is 81, at Manakiki. Twice.)

Future editions will be influenced by the response of readers. Cards and letters will be welcomed and carefully read.

The author is eager to meet the players who vowed this spring to *play the book* in a single season—especially those who made it.

CLEVELAND'S
Public Golf Courses
A Player's Guide

Airport Greens Golf Course
Willoughby Hills

Signage on most golf courses is limited to advising players where carts may not go. At Airport Greens, one sign reads, "Warning. This facility is used in FAA air traffic control. Loss of human life can occur from service interruption. Any person who interferes with air traffic control, or damages or trespasses on this property will be prosecuted under federal law."

This is what happens when a golf course is built on an airport. Dick LaConte, PGA, who designed the course on Cuyahoga County Airport turf, has mixed golf and aviation before. On the clubhouse wall is a copy of a 30-year-old newspaper story about LaConte crashing his light plane into a tree while photographing the 13th hole at the now-defunct Mayfield Heights Golf Club.

"I have to be one of few people alive to successfully land an airplane in a tree on a golf course," LaConte said. He is likely one of few course designers whose layouts share property with airplanes, too. "It's a combination of Scottish links in the open areas because we had the restrictions of the airport. The airport demands that we put nothing through the landing light system area. We can't plant trees there because we have a height restriction and we were restricted in the areas adjacent to the course. It's a unique piece of property."

No one is going to argue with that.

This new course opened in 1991. League players were waiting; teams from TRW, St. Luke's Hospital, Argotech, and Reliance Electric quickly signed up.

The club is too young to have golf stories, pro Steve Brzytwa pointed out, though the first death on the course occurred the second day of play. A gentleman with a four-year-old heart transplant died while putting on the 12th green. "Like a lot of golfers, he always said that if he had to go, he'd like to go on a golf course."

Like all new courses, it will take a few years of hard work to bring Airport Greens to maturity. The absence of topsoil, LaConte said, is a problem not yet resolved. Amenities will include a golf academy and instruction for beginners through advanced players.

In addition to a 40-seat clubhouse, Airport Greens has picnic grounds and will provide everything for outings. The pro shop here is well stocked and Brzytwa brags that he offers better prices than other shops. "You know, part of establishing a business is educating the golfer." Educated golfers report to him that the pro shop prices are quite good. They also tell him about the greens on the course. "They're amazed at our greens," he said. "They feel they're as good as a country club's." The irrigation system covers tees and fairways as well as greens. They were all in very rough shape for the inaugural year because of dry weather and the lack of topsoil.

"I'd call it a sporty golf course," Brzytwa said. It plays 5,230 yards, par 70. Not long, he said, but "It offers all the shots and a lot of challenge around the greens, mostly mounds. And it's a course that doesn't really need sand traps because it is that challenging." One challenge here is concentrating on the stroke while a Cessna takes off or lands.

The opening hole is a 295-yard par 4. The fairway is wide and bends softly to the right. Mounds on either side help define the hole. The fairway dips and rolls before arriving at a green elevated about 10 feet. No. 2, a 215-yard par 3, is an unusual hole for a short course described as "sporty"—a 215-yard par 3 is a pro-length hole. Double bogeys will be posted here far more often than pars. A culvert runs 75 yards in front of the green, which is surrounded by mounds.

No. 6 is a par 3, 170 yards. A hook on this tee will send the ball off the course and across Bishop Road. The green is substantial and players cross the county line—Cuyahoga/Lake—when walking from one end of the green to the other.

At No. 7 tee, the sign promising prosecution is attached to the door of a small building, used, obviously, for airport business. Landing lights mark the way to the tee. The hole is a 455-yard par 5, the number two handicap on this side. The tee here (as elsewhere on the course) is not well marked and a little shabby. That will probably change as the course matures, but Cleveland golfers are used to flower boxes, park bench seating, and handsome signs.

No. 9 is a sharp dogleg left. A mid-iron should suffice to reach the elbow. Gamblers will see decent odds in trying to cut the corner from the tee; in it are trees and mounds, but nothing insurmountable.

The last hole before crossing White Road and leaving the airport for a half-dozen holes is No. 10, one of three par 3s on the back side. From an elevated tee, a valley drops to the end of a narrow lake. The fairway then rises to the green, which is surrounded by mounds. Across the road, No. 11 is a straightaway par 4, measuring 270 yards. But suddenly the course is much more attractive. Grass on the fairways will do that. This doesn't alleviate the difficulties of playing with planes in the background (and foreground), however, and players with air combat experience will likely rise to the top.

The lone par 5 on this side is No. 12, a 450-yard hole that takes a soft dogleg right and then dips for a creek 80 yards in front of the green. From the 13th tee, the drive goes back over the same water that crossed the 12th fairway. It's a pretty hole, guided on both sides by hardwoods. The fairway crests slightly before bending left toward the green. There is sand on the left front of the green and a second creek running diagonally across the fairway from 20 to 80 yards out.

Nos. 17 and 18 are two finishing par 3s that play around a long and narrow lake. No. 17 plays 165 yards with the lake down its left side. For No. 18, players turn around and play 175 yards back to the clubhouse, water again on the left.

Airport Greens has a nice clubhouse and excellent pro shop. The location—the Cuyahoga County Airport—is puzzling. The course itself lacks topsoil, grass, and well-kept tee boxes. But with the guidance of Mr. LaConte, whose family has owned and operated golf courses for many years, the grass will grow and the course mature and fill its own niche.

Airport Greens Golf Course
28980 White Rd.
Willoughby, OH 44092   Phone: 944-6164

Owner: Gary LaConte
Manager: Laura LaConte

18 holes
Tees	Yds.	Course	Slope
Middle:	5230	64.8	101
Back:	5730	67.0	105
Forward:	4670	66.0	103

Season: Apr 1–Nov 15
Hours: 6 a.m.–10 p.m.
Greens fees: $7.00 / $13.00 wkdays; $8.00 / $15.00 wkends
Special rates: senior specials available
Carts: $8.50 / $16.00
Tee times: taken daily; recommended wkends
Practice facilities: range, putting greens, chipping green
Clubhouse facilities: food, beer, liquor
Outings: regular course events; private outings available
League play: wkday mornings and late afternoons
Pro shop: well stocked
Lessons: daily by appointment
Ranger: afternoons and wkends
New features: adding trees and bunkers

Astorhurst Country Club
Walton Hills

"I have them in boxes and catalogs. I have a clothes closet that I can't put any clothes in. They crowd my apartment," said Paul Tirpak, PGA, Director of Golf at Astorhurst. He was talking about his collection of score cards. More than 13,000 score cards. He's been collecting them for almost 30 years. "They're from all over." Friends who travel to clubs in the United States. and around the world contribute to the collection.

In addition to collecting scorecards, Tirpak provides lessons for both novices and advanced players. He also presides over a very busy course from a well-stocked, if crowded, pro shop. Leagues fill the course Monday through Thursday in the late afternoon and outings are popular on Fridays.

Astorhurst is a layout where virtually every hole is different. Not a long course (from the white tees 6,075 yards, par 71), it takes advantage of hilly terrain and, except for one corner of the course that gets too crowded, it is a handsome layout.

Tirpak said the greens are kept at 3/16" and the rough at a very rough 2 1/4". Fairways are mowed at 1/2". Small pines serve as markers at 150 and 100 yards.

No. 1, a 360-yard par 4, is a pine tree–lined hole with a late and sharp dogleg left. There is plenty of sand here and all over this course. The greens often slope and are generally fast.

No. 2 is an awesome 455-yard par 4. The tee to this number one handicap hole is reached by climbing aboard an old open tram and pushing a button. The metal cable underneath hauls players and bags more than 100 feet up the steep hillside. For players not familiar with the ride it can be unnerving, as the machinery rattles and groans. There is another route, a cart path cut into the side of the hill. This hole calls for a big drive but offers a wide fairway to land in. The terrain rises and falls as much as 20 feet. Halfway to the green the dogleg right begins, and in the right rough is an unusual set of sand traps. Not visible from the tee, they are five rectangular traps laid side to side—reminiscent of the famous "church pews" at Oakmont Country Club in Pennsylvania. There is more sand on the left side, but none at the green.

No. 4 is an especially difficult hole because of the shape and width of the fairway and because of the accuracy called for. A 365-yard par 4, its dogleg bends left about 170 yards from the green; the elbow is filled with hardwoods. The fairway measures 22 yards across there, and it rises quickly toward the green. Hitting through the fairway from the tee is not uncommon, and the ball continues into a valley.

No. 7 is the only par 5 on the front nine, 590 yards. Its tee looks out over a wide fairway and, off to the right, a practice area. Still, care must be taken in this, the crowded corner. A pulled tee shot can whistle over the heads of putters on the 5th green or drivers on the 6th tee. The 7th fairway drops from the tee and spreads out for the first few hundred yards. Then it takes a sharp dogleg to the right and rises about 10 feet. The flag is not visible for the second shot, and there is the chance of hitting through the fairway. Par is considered a fine score on this hole.

The tee at No. 8 may make players wish for a mulligan. It sits on a high cliff and looks out and down on fairway and lake. A great shot will clear the lake and follow the fairway as it travels to the right. The shot must also clear a pair of old oaks standing at the right side of the lake. They are easily 60 feet high with limbs 50 feet across. The approach shot is to an elevated green with sand on both sides. This 410-yard par 4 can provide play worth talking about in the clubhouse. It can also provide the setting for a disaster hole.

No. 9 looks easy on the scorecard, a par 4 of only 290 yards. But its narrow fairway has water down much of the right side and there is plenty of sand—four traps—at the green. A small creek cuts across the fairway.

No. 10 begins next to the No. 1 tee and the two briefly play next to each other. The right side of the hole is lined with pines. The fairway is not wide on this 290-yard par 4; there is a soft dogleg left and the green is slightly elevated. Behind it are mounds; to the left, sand.

To get to the next tee, players can board the tram or walk up the side of the hill. On exiting the tram, players must push a button to send it back down. Forgetting to send it down means players without riding carts are forced to walk up. Being forced to walk here is not a mood enhancer.

No. 12 is a handsome par 5 of 480 yards. Its fairway is wide, but rough on the right quickly leads out of bounds into thick woods. The fairway glides up and down before rising gently the final 50 yards to a green with sand and trees on both sides. No. 13, a par 3 that plays over the valley floor and a separate women's green, is a long and hazardous 180 yards. The difficulty here is more than clearing the deep valley; woods on either side, especially the right, can be very troublesome.

Nos. 14 and 15 play parallel. The first is a 320-yard par 4 that begins at an elevated tee. The view from it is particularly fine; it looks down on a wide fairway, hemmed on the right by a line of trees and on the left by dense woods. The green is protected on both sides by woods and, on the right, a narrow valley about 25 feet deep but only 25 or 30 feet across. It can't be seen for the foliage until the player reaches it. This green appears to have been carved out of the tree line.

No. 15, a 480-yard par 5, has a wide fairway. On the right side is the fairway from the previous hole. On the left are deep woods. From the tee, the fairway drops slowly to a valley and doesn't come back up until the last 150 yards. The approach on this hole is the most difficult shot. The green is substantially elevated and has trees on both sides. The fairway narrows near the green—only 21 yards across at the 75-yard mark.

The 16th tee completes a beautiful threesome. It is at a juncture of the 14th and 16th tees and the 15th green. While not crowded, this is a gathering place because it has a ball washer, rain shelter, and ice water. No. 16 is a 430-yard par 4, a straight and narrow hole. Deep woods on both sides make accuracy important here. The elevated green is protected with sand.

No. 18 is another spectacular tee. It sits on the edge of a cliff and looks out on this 490-yard par 5 shaped like the letter C. The right side is o.b. for the sake of safety; other fairways are there. Once the last magnificent tee shot has been launched, it's down a steep cart path. Nailed into a tree is a sign: "Speed Kills. Keep Cart Under Control." From here it is a flat hole to a flat green with sand traps on both sides.

The clubhouse, a one-story cement block building, offers standard fare. For big winners, next door is The Astorhurst Country Place, where dinner specials may include pork tenderloin marsala and pan-fried baby beef liver.

Astorhurst Country Club

Astorhurst Country Club
7000 Dunham Rd.
Cleveland, OH 44146   Phone: 439-3636

Director of Golf: Paul G. Tirpak, PGA
Pro: Douglas Smith, PGA

18 holes

Tees	Yds.	Course	Slope
Middle:	6075	69.1	118
Back:	6342	70.3	120
Forward:	5945	73.7	124

Season:	year 'round
Hours:	6 a.m.–10 p.m. (summer)
Greens fees:	$8.25 / $15.50 wkdays; $10.50 / $19.00 wkends & holidays
Special rates:	wkday special: $18.75 per person for 18 holes & 1/2 cart before 8 a.m. seniors (65 or older): $14.75 for 18 holes & 1/2 cart before 3 p.m. wkdays family, single, senior, & driving range memberships available
Carts:	$9.50 / $16.75
Tee times:	taken daily, up to 2 days in advance (7 days with credit card)—cancel by 48 hrs. in advance or be charged
Practice facilities:	putting green, chipping green
Clubhouse facilities:	food, beer, liquor; private rooms
Outings:	private outings welcomed wkdays & wkends
League play:	various times
Pro shop:	well stocked
Lessons:	$25.00 per 1/2 hr., daily
Ranger:	daily
Special rules:	carts mandatory until 10 a.m. wkends & holidays
New features:	150 newly planted trees; renovation of traps

Auburn Springs Country Club
Chagrin Falls

"Men are usually wild," manager Evelyn Weese says, "they go everywhere." She was explaining high scores on this course. And she knows what she's talking about—Weese turns in scores in the mid-80s on a regular basis. "On the front there's a lot of water and in the back a lot of woods. If you hit a straight ball, you're okay."

The course was built in the late sixties on farmland. Ernie Mizda is the builder and owner. He owned a century home near the road for many years but it was set afire a couple of years ago. Weese's bag of clubs was destroyed. The clubs were easily replaced, she said, but not so the violin collection of Mr. Mizda—there were about 140 in the house. The arson case has never been solved.

The golf course is a tough one, a bit rough around the edges as well. The men and women who show up at the cashier's desk are here only to play golf. The club has a "basics-only" pro shop. No driving range here, and no rangers on the course. There isn't any pro on the staff and no lessons are provided. Tee times are taken for weekend play. Mizda has two noteworthy rules on the scorecard: no one under 21 may drive a golf cart, and beginners are not allowed on the course during busy periods.

No. 1 is a 375-yard par 4 that begins from an elevated tee. The fairway drops down to the left. Plenty of players try to cut the dogleg because hitting straight can send a ball through the fairway. There are trees down the left side and a small pond, too. Behind the well-maintained green is a second pond.

No. 2 is a 490-yard par 5 that starts rising and doesn't stop rising until it approaches the green. It plays much longer than the listed 490 yards. A snap hook off this tee will send a ball into a small lake about 100 yards out. The left side here is thick woods. Down the right side, the hole is marked by a big willow and a line of trees.

No. 5 is a par 5 of 480 yards with two water hazards. The second, in front of the green, is guarded by a ceramic frog.

Three tough par 4s finish the side—two of them 440-yarders. No. 7, the number three handicap hole, is a big dogleg left. On the way into the green a long mound sits on the right side; beyond the mound is water. But failing to play the right side of the fairway here can mean an especially difficult approach shot, because a stand of trees sits at the left front of the green. Still farther to the left is another pond.

No. 8, 370 yards, is another dogleg, almost 90 degrees to the right. At the turn, luxury homes line the left side. The tee at No. 9 has a gazebo—a rain shelter, actually, but a rustic and pretty touch. The hole is rated the number one handicap. Except for its length, though, it doesn't provide much opportunity for heroics or much memorable architecture. Still, for the average player to par a 440-yard par 4—that's heroic and memorable enough.

No. 13 is a 352-yard par 4. A big dogleg right, players might be tempted to cut it. But in the corner of the turn is a stand of very tall hardwoods. At the 150-yard marker (these are discs in the center of fairways), the fairway turns and the left side becomes o.b. There is no sand at the green, but there is the matter of a pond in the front left of the green.

No. 17 is a par 5—570 yards that bend constantly to the right. About halfway to the green there is a small lake on the right side. This is a workingman's par 5; it calls for nothing fancy, only three solid, straight shots to cover the yardage and avoid the hazards.

After putting out on No. 18 and heading for the clubhouse, players run into the original Paul Bunyan driver. It is almost 15 feet tall, carved of two large pieces of wood with a black grip, brown shaft, and black hosel. It arrived about ten years ago when one of the company teams in league play received it from players in the parent company. They asked Mizda if it might rest at his course.

Auburn Springs has the charm of a country picnic. It is not a course that stands on ceremony. This comes from the owner, whose personality is reflected in his course. It certainly adds to the variety of golf available here.

Auburn Springs Country Club
10001 Stafford Rd.
Chagrin Falls, OH 44022   Phone: 543-4448

Owner: Ernie Mizda

18 holes

Tees	Yds.	Course	Slope
Middle:	6543	70.3	112
Back:	6874	71.9	117
Forward:	5530	70.7	113

Season: year-round
Hours: sunrise–sunset
Greens fees: $7.00 / $12.00
Special rates: $30.00 for 18 holes w/ cart, restricted days & times
                         seniors: $27.00 for 18 holes w/ cart, restricted days & times
Carts: $9.00 / $17.00
Tee times: taken wkends only
Practice facilities: putting green
Clubhouse facilities: food, beer, liquor; private rooms
Outings: available
League play: Mon–Fri 4:00 p.m.–dark; Wed all day
Pro shop: lightly stocked
Lessons: not available
Ranger: daily
New features: adding traps, trees, and fairway water; driving range under construction

Avondale Golf Club
Avon

George Nolan built the front side of Avondale on farmland and opened it for play in 1974. It was his dream to operate the course in his retirement; he had the back nine sketched when he succumbed to a heart attack. His sons built the back nine and today run the operation with their mother, Jane Noll. "It became a family affair," Al Nolan said.

He and his brother George took delivery last year of a trencher—trusting Mother Nature to deliver rain in a timely manner leads lots of owners to disappointment. Avondale is putting in irrigation. And every year more drainage tiles are added. When a few lakes were built recently, the excavated dirt was turned into mounds that line both fairway and rough and make Avondale a course difficult to score well on.

There is some variety in the greens here: a couple are two-tiered, a few are small or unusually shaped (pin placement on the par 3 16th can mean a putt as long as 120 feet), more are big. Many are surrounded by sand and mounds. They are all kept in excellent condition. "That's what we're noted for," Al Nolan said. "They're the best greens in the county," he added, a boast made by many owners.

The clubhouse is small, though a pavilion comfortably holds 200 for outings. The snack bar serves the usual golfer fare. There is league play every day of the week, so calling for tee times is always a good idea.

This is a flat course made interesting with the mounds and man-made lakes. The back side is tighter and much prettier than the ex-farm front because it was carved out of oak forest.

There are electric lines cutting through the course, especially on the front side; the holes were designed to avoid them.

Landing near them is no penalty; a two-club length drop is offered.

No. 1 is a par 5 of 500 yards. Three mounds in the middle of the fairway confront players on the tee and more mounds come into play for the second shot. The approach must take into account the lake and the sand to the right of the green. For first-time players this can be a hectic opening hole.

No. 2, a dogleg right, has a lake along the right side. On this 370-yard par 4, staying in the fairway is important. Off to the left, drives can end up on or behind mounds. A small lake sits on the right side of this dogleg right.

No. 3, a par 3 of 175 yards, is one of many holes studied by Al Nolan. When scoring for outings, he sees more high scores on this hole than any else. Although it is technically the number 15 handicap, he says it plays the hardest. "It's always playing into the wind and most people are short of the green," he explained. Short of the green there is trouble where mounds protect the front. Off to the right is a small pond and on the right side of the green, sand.

Holes No. 4, 5, and 6 play parallel to each other. Golfers on the 4th tee can cut across the 5th fairway to get to the green. No. 4 is a 360-yard par 4, a dogleg left. In the corner of the turn, The Pit was built. This is a mound with a pit in the middle. The corner can still be cut, but only by big and accurate hitters. Missing it and playing the second shot from The Pit will likely add at least one stroke. There is sand beside the green, behind which sits a sizable pond.

No. 7 bends to the left; on the right are a couple of lakes. It is a 465-yard par 5 with three traps at the green, which is surrounded by mounds. No. 8 is only 140 yards, but this par 3 often plays into the wind and players coming up short find themselves climbing over one of the rolling mounds before the green.

The last hole on the front side is a 370-yard par 4. A fairway trap at about 230 yards out slows the roll of some drives. This hole has a generous green to shoot at.

Avondale Golf Club

No. 10 is a short par 4, only 340 yards, and despite mounds on the left side of the fairway and sand on the left side of the green, it is a wide open hole. No. 11 is just the opposite—narrow, with o.b. on the right and trees on both sides. A par 4 of 390 yards, it has a big green with a trap on the left side.

No. 12, a par 4 of 365 yards, has three pot bunkers waiting at 210 yards on the right side of the fairway. The hole also has the toughest green on the course, including a two-tiered putting surface and a pair of sand traps.

The only par 5 on this side is No. 13, a 470-yard hole that tempts players to reach for the green in two. "It doesn't get eagled very often," Al Nolan said. The hole bends to the left and getting on in two calls for clearing a few 50-foot oaks en route. If that shot leaks to the right, it will end up in a pond close to the green.

No. 15, a 308-yard par 4 is a dogleg right with four fairway traps to clear. Big hitters going for the green in one usually find their balls in the last trap. There is more sand at the green, which is small.

No. 16, par 3, 160 yards, has plenty of water to carry. And the long and narrow green is no piece of cake, either. This is the hole that provides the club with the most used golf balls. No. 17 is a 325-yard par 4 that is lined with mounds and dotted with fairway sand. The biggest trap stretches across the whole front of the green, so no rolling them on here.

The finishing hole has water in front of the tee. The drive on this 375-yard par 4, the only uphill hole here, has to carry a large pond. The green is two-tiered and sand lines both sides. The putting surface has plenty of action to it and for reasons not clear is faster than others here. "It's a knee-knocker," Nolan said.

The late George Nolan would be proud of the current Avondale. His dream golf course is well tended by his widow and sons; they continue to improve and refine it.

Avondale Golf Club
38490 Detroit Rd.
Avon, OH 44011   Phone: 835-5836, Cleve.; 934-4398, Lorain

Owner: E. Jane Noll

18 holes
Tees   Yds.   Course   Slope
Middle: 5993   68.5   116
Back: 6263   69.9   118
Forward: 5400   70.7   114

Season: year-round
Hours: 5:30 a.m.–10:00 p.m.
Greens fees: $6.25 / $12.00 wkdays; $6.75 / $13.00 wkends, holidays
Special rates: seniors: $5.00 / $9.50 wkdays until 2 p.m.
                        seniors: $15.50 for 18 holes and 1/2 cart
                        annual membership available
Carts: $8.00 / $16.00 plus tax
Tee times: taken, not required
Practice facilities: putting green
Clubhouse facilities: snack bar: food, beer, liquor
Outings: catered events; seating for 200; pavilion
League play: various times
Pro shop: well stocked
Lessons: by appointment
Ranger: daily
New features: adding full fairway irrigation system; adding more women's tees; adding blue tee to No. 13

Berkshire Hills Country Club
Chesterland

If a player wanted to argue that Berkshire Hills is the most beautiful course in the area, he would find plenty of supporting evidence between the 1st tee and the 18th green. The course is only about 30 years old and was designed by Ben Zink, who also designed the layout for Landerhaven. Landerhaven was a prairie without features; Berkshire is a roller coaster without tracks.

The winding and hilly drive from State Route 322 to the parking lot is much like the course itself: lined with trees and given to following the terrain.

The clubhouse is like an old family album: battered a bit, but treasured. Tee times are taken for weekend and holiday mornings. To play at other times, just show up. Ron Miesz, who runs the course, keeps only basics in his pro shop. There is a driving range and a practice green, and Berkshire staffs a teaching professional.

On the other side of the clubhouse is the dining facility for outings: an old dairy barn. It is a splendid setting for prime rib and cloth napkins. Friday is the day for outings there.

Berkshire is a well manicured and maintained course and few starting holes match the grandeur of its No. 1. This par 5, 537-yard dogleg begins by sweeping down from the tee, then veers up and to the right. In the elbow of the dogleg is a large lake. It is a rare player who tries to clear the lake with a tee shot; the fairway is wide, the rough easily playable. When the sky is clear but for a few clouds, the view here belongs on a picture postcard.

The big, round green at No. 1 has a couple of slender traps on either side, traps that wrap around the perimeter. This type of trap will be seen the rest of the round.

No. 2 is straightaway for about as far as a 3-wood will send the ball. Then this 340-yard par 4 takes an abrupt right turn near the 150-yard marker and the fairway dips slightly. The approach shot is to a green at the end of a hallway of old, stately trees. And behind the green stand a half-dozen tall evergreens. The walk to No. 3 tee is through woods that are tall and so thick that sunlight does not make it to the the path, which is covered with moss.

No. 4 is another par 5, this one a 505-yard uphill hole that will likely confuse the first-time player. A pond rests in front of the tee and the drive must be straight. As throughout the course, old hardwoods line the fairway and stand ready to slap down errant shots. More than accuracy is called for here; good scores are often posted by long hitters. The fairway rises towards an aiming flag, where it crests and then rolls straight to the green. The green is half-surrounded in the rear by heavy, heavy brush.

No. 7 is the number one handicap hole, a 448-yard par 4 that demands a straight hit from the elevated tee and an approach shot of much accuracy and length. The fairway rises and dips more than once before nearing the green, where the left side of the fairway precipitously drops off.

No. 9 is 403 yards, a par 4 with a blind tee shot to a wide fairway. On the right side of the fairway is a bell—a couple of strikes signals the players on the tee when it is safe for them to hit. The hole has a big, welcoming green with a little sand on either side and a white rail fence behind, along the road. It's a good hole to turn around on and enjoy a perspective golfers often miss—golf holes can be just as gorgeous from the green looking back to the tee as from tee to green.

Some golfers may choose to go directly to the 10th tee rather than stop for refreshment at the clubhouse; for all the beauty and challenge of the front side, the back side is more beautiful and more challenging. Furthermore, a cart patrols the course and carries a cooler filled with cold beer and soft drinks.

Berkshire Hills Country Club

No. 10, a 252-yard par 4, goes up. And up. And up. It's not a difficult hole, if players stay on the straight and narrow. If the ball strays left, it finds deep woods. Trees protect the front and right of the green, though even those not known for their length off the tee might be able to drive it.

With No. 12 begin what may be the four best consecutive holes in northern Ohio. No. 12 is a 453-yard par 4 that takes a ride through the woods the Headless Horseman wouldn't consider. The tee shot, ideally a soft draw, has to go uphill and slightly left. Deep forest lines the left and plenty of maples and pin oaks line the right. Starting at the 150-yard marker the fairway descends rapidly, crosses water, and finally comes to the green.

The next tee, No. 13, presents a target only a couple dozen yards wide. The tee shot has to go almost straight uphill and, at the crest, trees close in on both sides. This 472-yard par 5 plays down a snug fairway.

No. 14 is a 360-yard par 4, which sounds easy, but this hole calls for careful shotmaking—especially the approach to the green, which is slight elevated.

No. 15 is a par 5, 509-yard hole that bends right, falls to a creek, then rises sharply up and left to the green. Play outside of the short grass makes this hole especially tough. The walk through the woods to the next tee is a good time to catch one's breath; some interesting golf is played in those last four holes.

The 18th hole looks like it was designed by Andrew Wyeth. From a small, even private tee box, across a sparkling lake, the hole is a 135-yard par 3. The green has water on three sides, and to the rear the ground rises dramatically. Players who are walking get to stroll across the wooden foot bridge from tee to green. (Carts must use a more substantial bridge.) The water, the waving flag on its white pole, and the green make for a beautiful finishing hole. It's almost as if the architect decided to comfort the players after their round.

Berkshire is a long course: 6,346 for par 72. The blue tees take the course to 6,607, par 73. The women's tees were not provided as an afterthought; they are well built and maintained, and they provide reasonable advantage. Water fountains and telephones for emergency use dot the course.

This is a great course for hosting out-of-town guests unfamiliar with the quality of courses available here.

Berkshire Hills Country Club
9760 Mayfield Rd.
Chesterland, OH 44026   Phone: 729-9516

Manager: Ray Petty, PGA

Tees	Yds.	Course	Slope
Middle:	6346	71.0	127
Back:	6607	72.1	129
Forward:	5512	71.8	122

Season: year-round
Hours: sunrise–sunset
Greens fees ('91): $7.00 / $13.00 wkdays; $9.50 / $17.00 wkends
Special rates: seniors: 18 holes & cart, $17 per person (wkdays only)
Carts: $8.50 / $16.00
Tee times: taken wkends
Practice facilities: driving range, putting green
Clubhouse facilities: snack bar: food, soft drinks, no liquor
Outings: Fridays, dinners served in the barn
League play: Mon–Fri
Pro shop: lightly stocked
Lessons: by appointment
Ranger: daily
Other: soft drinks, beer are offered on course
New features: rebuilt tee on No. 18, improvements on 3 additional tees; the prettiest fishing hole in the state; improved cart paths

Big Met Public Golf Course
Fairview Park

This Metroparks course has been a West Side favorite for a couple of generations of golfers. It is an attractive and playable course, and so conveniently located that getting there for many is a matter of ten or fifteen minutes. When play is light, it is a matter of ten or fifteen minutes from home to the *first tee*. This convenience has a downside, however. There are days when the parking lot overflows with cars and the wait to tee off can be excruciating. The course plays very slowly on such days.

Slow play is a dilemma for which there seems to be no solution. Gunplay works, but not everyone packs a pistol. Tom Haley, the veteran television personality, plays here often; one day his foursome included a Cleveland police officer. The course was crowded and play was slow, but the foursome in front of Mr. Haley was criminally slow. Frustrated with having no opportunity to develop a tempo for the match, the cop drew a .45 automatic from his bag and fired two shots in the air. He also shouted at the foursome, questioning the heritage of the members and insisting they play faster. Of the incident, Mr. Haley says, "Trust me. It happened. I had my back to the guy when he let go with the .45. It got *my* attention. And we never saw that group ahead of us again."

Developing and encouraging golf etiquette is important, especially at a course where more than 50,000 rounds are played every year. Many players here fail to break 100 and the quality of play, combined with the number of rounds, brings a great deal of pressure to the course. That Mel Ferencik, the soft-spoken manager, is able to keep the course in such good shape speaks well of his staff.

There are no facilities here for outings, and Metroparks policy is to reserve every third tee time for walk-on players. Players are expected to know their way around the course and no information about the holes is posted at the tees. Only recently were 150-yard markers installed.

This is not a difficult course, though there are tough holes on it. Sitting in the Rocky River Reservation, known as "the valley" to West Siders, this essentially flat layout provides great physical beauty to players. There are animals in addition to pistol-packing Cleveland cops at Big Met, including a pair of red fox and dozens of deer. A minor inconvenience is provided by planes leaving and arriving at Hopkins Airport, just south of the course.

The first hole is a 403-yard par 4 with a generous fairway, which is often ignored by players who slice their drives into the adjacent No. 2 green. It is a straight hole calling for two long shots. The fairway is lined on the right with small trees, mostly pines. Except for a stand of tall hardwoods, the left side is open. There is sand at the left side of the green. The greens on this course are neither tricky nor fast but they hold approach shots well and are always in very good shape.

No. 5, the first par 5, measures 452 yards and includes a dogleg left near the green. Again, it's a wide open fairway. At one time a huge tree stood in the elbow of this dogleg. Lightning eliminated that hazard. More trees have been planted there, however, and as time goes on the hole will narrow. The rear of the green rises; behind, ground topples over into the Rocky River. Losing a ball to the river was always an acceptable hazard on this hole. That's no longer true. The grounds staff has draped a bright orange plastic fence behind the green at the edge of the water. Pilots passing over probably check for smoking wreckage and survivors. This method of saving a few golf balls is unnecessary, unnatural, and ugly.

No. 7 is one of the signature holes at Big Met. It's a par 5 of 500 yards. From the tee, trees mark the sides of the fairway as it heads straight for the woods and the river. It bends sharply left and follows the river's edge to the green. Cutting the corner from the tee is a dangerous proposition; the elbow is filled with tall trees and also the elevated green of the next hole. After the bend, trees line the left side and the terrain is slightly hilly. A huge green slopes slightly forward. To the left of the green, the ground falls off sharply to a marshy area.

No. 9, a par 4 of 405 yards, is beautiful for the woods that line the right side and the stand of trees on the left. The green is raised to about 10 feet and is mounded on three sides. At its base, on the right side, is a huge hardwood.

Andy Michnay, Bible student and long time golfer, has been playing Big Met for almost 60 years. When he began playing, green fees were 50 cents for 18 holes. Many years ago, he was playing the front side with a friend, a good golfer having a bad day. When he reached this tree at the bottom of the 9th green, Michnay's friend began destroying his clubs. He took them, one after the other, and wrapped the shaft around the tree, muttering the whole time, "I gotta get offa this course, I gotta get offa this course." Like so many players, though, he was unable to stop at the turn. "He played the back side out of my bag and shot a 35," Michnay said.

The layout was different when Michnay first played. Today's 11th hole was No. 1 back then. "At the tee, we had a pail of sand and a pail of water. We just used sand for tees. And the water was for washing clubs or balls."

Though he has fired four aces over the course of his amateur career, Michnay's vision is very poor today. Playing partners often place a white coffee cup behind the hole so he can see where he's putting. His clubs have been relabeled with extra-large numbers. Jerome McGinty, who often plays with Michnay, said, "Once he gets lined up and hits the ball, he can see in his mind's eye where the ball's going. I've asked him to play other courses, but he won't play anyplace but here. He really does know it like the back of his hand."

No. 11 is a pretty par 4, 365 yards from an elevated tee to a wide and straight fairway. Along the right side of the fairway the ground rises 15 feet then drops to the river, which continues alongside the next few holes. The left side is lined with trees.

No. 14 is certainly the most difficult hole on the course, even though No. 9 is designated the number one handicap. At 424 yards, it's a long par 4. A dogleg right turns around the 150-yard mark. To score well on this hole calls for a pro-length drive and great second shot. If the drive leaves the ball on the right side, trees in the elbow of the dogleg will prevent a clear approach. And the green itself is tricky; it is egg-shaped and has steep sides. It's not unusual to land a ball on the green only to watch it roll right off.

No. 16, a par 5 of 474 yards, is lined with trees all the way down the right side. Until the last 150 yards, trees line the left side as well. From a tee shrouded with oaks, maples, and ashes, the fairway rises slightly and runs for a hundred yards before dropping five or six feet and leveling out for the finish of the hole.

The final two holes are short par 4s more at home on an executive-length course than here. No. 17 is a straight, 289-yard hole with a plateau in the fairway and plenty of room. Big hitters who are also big slicers, however, can land on the 18th tee. No. 18, 293 yards slightly uphill toward the clubhouse, has a mound in front of the green that makes judging the approach shot difficult.

There are occasional surprises on the course. Sometimes a pair of red foxes will raise eyebrows as they take their evening walk. Or a heron swooping down to stand in a marsh will hush a foursome. But Big Met is mostly comfortable and familiar, like starter Mike McLaughlin. The skinny Irishman has a big smile, a steady tenor, and a willingness to accommodate the needs of public golfers; he's one of the many reasons Big Met does such a big business.

Big Met Public Golf Course

Big Met Public Golf Course
4811 Valley Pkwy.
Fairview Park, OH 44126   Phone: 331-1070

Manager: Mel Ferencik

18 holes
Tees	Yds.	Course	Slope
Middle:	6085	68.0	108
Forward:	5870	72.0	113

Season: Mar 18–Nov 25
Hours: sunrise–sunset
Greens fees: $7.00 / $13.00
Special rates: seniors: $5.00 / $10.00 wkdays
Carts: $8.50 / $17.00
Tee times: taken, not required
Practice facilities: putting green
Clubhouse facilities: snack bar: food, beer
Outings: available
League play: various times
Pro shop: well stocked; Mar 18–Nov 25
Lessons: not available
Ranger: daily

Big Springs Golf Club
Hudson

Long before Big Springs was a tough little golf course, it was a campground for Native Americans. The name comes from the springs in the northeast corner of the course. The club logo is an arrowhead.

Owner/developer Ralph Obert, Sr. opened the course in 1975, three years after incorporating with partner Richard Peniston. "We had more drive than expertise, actually," he says today. The two met in 1966 when a group of businessmen were drafting plans to build Hudson Country Club. "He was quite a golf enthusiast and I was business oriented. We talked about getting together and building a public course."

But Mr. Peniston died shortly after Big Springs opened. "So I got interested in golf not from a golf standpoint, but from a business standpoint, and business is good," Obert said.

He described his course as moderately difficult. The average score here hovers around 100. After playing the course, it's easy to see how triple-digit scores can be posted. "It gives you a little bit of everything," Obert said, "uphill, downhill, sidehill, length, dense trees."

The course record was set by a former employee. "Our first employee, actually. William Bonar was a school teacher and we hired him in 1976, and he worked for us for about ten years. He was strictly amateur, but a super golfer," Obert said. In 1980, Bonar played from the blues, which make the course 6,466 yards, par 72, and turned in 32-34.

Tee times are taken only on weekends and holidays. Obert maintains minimum stock in his pro shop and explained, "We don't try to get into the golf equipment business any more. It's too competitive." No outings here; Obert finds them to be uncivilized. But there is league play.

They play with a passion that amazes Obert's wife, Jean. She still marvels at the conduct of one foursome that had a member take a seat on a bench and abruptly die. Cardiac arrest killed him. The foursome continued play, though as a threesome. "When golfers get out on that course, they forget everything," she said.

The husband and wife combination maintains course and clubhouse that are a couple of steps above average. The amenities include decorations for holidays, even Halloween. On the first tee, a flower bed blooms with half a dozen varieties.

No. 1 is a par 4, 385 yards. From the tee, the fairway drops slightly and bends to the right. It's a narrow fairway—only 23 yards wide at the 150-yard marker. The yardage markers are red 4 x 4s with white numerals. Obert keeps the grass at 5/8" on the fairway and only 3/16" on the green. The rough is a short 1 1/2". The greens are moderately fast.

No. 2 is a par 5, a 506-yard hole that plays straight but narrow. It rises gently with woods along the left side. On the right are remnants of an apple orchard. Two hundred yards from the green, the short fairway grass turns to rough for 40 yards, then back to fairway. At the green, trees close in on either side.

The number one handicap hole is No. 3, a 406-yard par 4. It is sandwiched between Nos. 4 and 7, but trees are well used to define the hole and it doesn't feel crowded. It's a narrow landing area for the drive here; the fairway is only 24 yards across. An ability to read subtlety in greens is valuable here.

The No. 4 tee looks down a fairway marked by natural beauty; a good example of how rolling terrain can be used to make a beautiful hole. A par 4, 377 yards, it begins from an elevated tee. There are woods on the horizon and down the right side. Also down the right side is o.b. The fairway on this dogleg right is wider than on previous holes.

This layout is a healthy blend of straight holes and doglegs, almost all of them narrow. Few are more narrow at the 150-yard marker than No. 7, a 325-yard par 4, where the fairway width is a skinny 16 yards. Of course, 325 yards is not very long, so many players leave their woods in the bag on this tee. It's a straightaway hole and deceptively pretty. From the elevated tee, everything is visible, but nothing looks threatening. Make a mistake here, however, and the course promptly exacts a penalty.

From the No. 8 tee, players can glance around and watch players on two other tees and one green. The economical use of the land is a source of pride for Obert. It's a long par 3, 198 yards from an elevated tee. The fairway drops immediately in front of the tee, then climbs to the green. Another very pretty hole, hardwoods define the fairway. The green is a difficult one, plenty of pitch and roll.

No. 9, a 477-yard par 5, has a softly snaking fairway. It swings to the right and then back to the left and up. Two hundred yards from the green there is sand on the right side. At about 130 yards, sand rests on both sides of the fairway. The narrow fairway is made more difficult by culverts near the green. On both sides, soft slices or soft hooks will result in a tough pitch to the green.

The back nine begins with another par 5, a 480-yard hole that rises, falls, and meanders out to a dogleg left. Hardwoods hem in both sides and water cuts into the fairway just before the green.

No. 11 is another pretty hole. This par 4, only 285 yards, bends down out to the left, then back up to the right. A pair of sizable sand traps bracket the fairway near the green. This green is particularly fast and unforgiving.

No. 16, a 160-yard par 3, is all water. The tee is on top of the built-up bank of the lake and a surprise for first-time players. The water is not visible until the 15-foot climb is completed. The green here slants forward and is backed by sand.

"Probably the best hole on the course is No. 17," says Obert. "Most of the club championships have been settled there." It is lined with thick woods on the left side. There are trees on the right; putting any of them between the ball and the green pretty much destroys any chance of par. The length of the hole dictates the difficulty. At 422 yards over softly hilly fairway, two big, accurate shots are called for. Launching an approach shot over the green sends the ball down into thick underbrush.

Big Springs is a tight course that doesn't look tight, a great course to walk and carry, a course that calls for thinking before swinging.

Big Springs Golf Club
1101 Barlow Rd.
Hudson, OH 44236   Phone: 656-2103, Cleve.; 655-2267, Akron

Owner: Ralph E. Obert, Sr.

18 holes

Tees	Yds.	Course	Slope
Middle:	6161	69.0	n/r
Back:	6456	70.5	n/r
Forward:	5167	65.9	n/r

Season: early Mar–early Dec
Hours: 6:30 a.m.–sunset
Greens fees: $8.00 / $14.00 wkdays; $10.00 / $18.00 wkends, holidays
Special rates: seniors, juniors: $6.75 / $10.00 wkdays
Carts: $8.50 / $17.00
Tee times: required wkends, holidays
Practice facilities: putting green, chipping area
Clubhouse facilities: food, beer, liquor
Outings: weekend groups only
League play: various times
Pro shop: lightly stocked
Lessons: not available
Ranger: yes

Black Brook Country Club
Mentor

The tee markers here are carved granite. It is an elegant touch and in keeping with Mary Lou Colbow's affectionate regard for the game. The president and manager of Black Brook comes from a golfing family; her father, Robert Shave, was the pro at Manakiki when it was a private club.

Colbow is a player of some repute and a student and fan of the game. Black Brook, she said, invests heavily in its junior program. Young players who are taught the game and its etiquette will likely always be grateful. Just as important, they will fill courses with golfers who play fast and well, and who take care of the course as they use it. In addition to the junior program, individual and group lessons are offered here.

The course is open all year and play is permitted according to the weather. Colbow said, "It's a good course for everybody. It's not super long, but it's not short and it has a lot of challenge in it—the back nine, especially, because it's tight." The greens are consistently fast and the course very well maintained.

Leagues fill the tees from 3 to 6 every weekday afternoon and about 200 kids show up on Friday mornings to learn the game. Tees, greens, and fairways are watered. The rough is left to fend for itself.

No. 1 is a nice introduction to the course. This 348-yard par 4 has a wide fairway and a line of trees down the right side. Off to the left is a small lake and an equipment shed. Babycakes, a one-eyed dog of dubious heritage, makes his home here and rarely strays from members of the ground crew. Neither lake nor shed should come into play.

No. 2, a 356-yard par 4, heads back toward the clubhouse. It starts straight out, then dips and bends left. Off to the right is a fence and o.b. A hundred yards from the green, the fairway drops as a creek cuts across it. On the right front corner of the green is a large sand trap.

The fence continues down the right edge of No. 3, a 344-yard par 4 that sits in the corner of the property. While the right is o.b., there is plenty of room in the wide fairway and open rough on the left. Much sand on this hole slows balls from bouncing left into the No. 8 tee or right to the fence. Players cross Lake Shore Boulevard to get to the next four holes.

No. 4 is the only par 5 on the front side and at 444 yards, it is not a long one. Still, for most players it will take three shots to reach the green. There is plenty of room to fit a slice before reaching the white o.b. stakes on the right side. This hole has one of the tougher greens. Plenty of sand around and in front of it, so rolling the ball on is not possible. The green itself has tough hills. It is easy enough to three-putt this hole (maybe more), so par here is a fine score.

No. 5 is a tree-lined par 4 of 377 yards. The narrow fairway plays in a shallow valley. The rough here will prevent almost any shot but chipping back to the fairway, and there is sand at the green on this number two handicap hole.

No. 6, a 371-yard par 4, is another tree-lined hole, this one with fairway sand at the 150-yard marker and more sand at the green. On the far right side here and on the next hole, houses and backyards provide a minor distraction.

The last three holes on the front side get shorter as they get closer to the clubhouse. No. 7, a 331-yard par 4, leads to the road, where a custard stand operates behind the green. Across the road, No. 8 is a 167-yard par 3. The green has a grass bunker in front and some sand on the left front. It is another green with potential for adventure. No. 9 is another par 3, this one only 150 yards.

The back side is slightly longer and more difficult. The terrain changes are marked by shallow and not-so-shallow valleys and much more water. The toughest hole is saved for last.

No. 10, though, is a short par 4—only 284 yards. It starts at an elevated tee overlooking a valley. Water crosses the valley but it's close enough to the tee that it shouldn't come into play. A pair of irons is all that's needed to get home here. No. 11, a 185-yard par 3, turns around and plays parallel to the previous hole. It's a gorgeous hole, calling for a big iron shot over valley and creek to a good-sized green. Sand at the green will prevent big hits from bouncing into the woods behind the green.

No. 12 is another challenge. A 406-yard par 4, it goes back across the valley. It drops right in front of the tee box and then rises and continues to rise until about 130 yards from the green, where it crests and falls slightly. Woods come in on the left side and make the approach shot more risky. And there is a grass bunker in front of this green.

No. 15 is a long par 4, 398 yards, with trees on both sides of the fairway. At this green, there is not only sand but an old, old maple tree that hangs over the edge on the left side. For players who used too much club for the approach shot, there is water to the left and rear. A wooden bridge over a creek leads to the next tee.

No. 17 is a picture-perfect par 3 of 150 yards. It is a hallway of hardwoods to a hilly green decorated on both sides by sand. And No. 18, the most challenging hole on the course, is equally beautiful. The tee shot on this 425-yard par 4 is blind; players have to go out a hundred yards to see the green. There are only a few trees on both sides, but the target area for the drive is not large. A straight hole, it starts dropping about 200 yards from the green. On the right of the valley floor is a lake. The terrain rises quickly to a green with three traps and deep woods behind it. Separating the woods from the green is a split rail fence.

Black Brook is an old and old-fashioned layout with holes that can delight the average player and holes that can confound. It is a little gem, off the side of the road, where management's commitment to the game is clearly evident.

Black Brook Country Club
8900 Lake Shore Blvd.
Mentor, OH 44060   Phone: 951-0010

| Manager: | Mary Lou Colbow |
| Pro: | Tim Ausperk |

18 holes

Tees	Yds.	Course	Slope
Middle:	5870	68.0	116
Back:	6123	69.1	118
Forward:	5398	70.5	117

Season:	year-round
Hours:	8:00 a.m.–5:00 p.m. winter
	6:00 a.m.–10:00 p.m. summer
Greens fees:	$7.25 / $13.25
Special rates:	2 people w/cart $40.00, wkdays
	seniors: 2 people w/cart $33.00, wkdays
Carts:	$9.00 / $18.00
Tee times:	taken wkends
Practice facilities:	range, putting green
Clubhouse facilities:	food, beer; pavilion
Outings:	cater all types, from 25–300
League play:	weekday mornings and afternoons
Pro shop:	well stocked; year-round
Lessons:	$25.00/ 1/2 hr.
Ranger:	daily
New features:	blue tees being lengthened 400 yds.

Bob-O-Link Golf Course
Avon

Three brothers, Michiganders, originally owned Bob-O-Links. Their business was not golf, but sod. They were trying to get out of the sod business but found themselves unable to get the price they wanted, so they turned the sod farm into a golf course. They had used this technique successfully before to sell land in Michigan. "They operated it for eight or nine years before I bought it along with two other partners in 1977. Basically, they were just maintaining it. They made no improvements or anything," said owner Bill Fitch.

Quite a bit has changed since then. The course now features 27 holes (all watered), three pavilions (one totally enclosed), 85 riding carts, a driving range, and a rule that should appear on all scorecards: Rule No. 9, under Local Rules, reads, "This is a fun game; play with courtesy."

More than 40 leagues play here, where the average score is 48 to 50 strokes for nine holes. A great outing business is done on Wednesdays and Saturdays. The new clubhouse, built in 1986, is roomy and comfortable and includes the pro shop, which carries the essentials only. Weather permitting, play continues all year.

Fitch has a good story about his first foursome. The original owners of the course gave to this foursome the keys to the clubhouse. They were always out playing before the owners showed up. They even made coffee for the owners. The foursome played together steadily from 1969. Two members of the foursome are dead now, both killed by heart attacks. "One was on the 14th hole and one was on the 16th," Fitch said. "The coincidence of that happening. . . ." The survivors continue to play.

Bob-O-Link Golf Course

The nines are designated by colors. The Red Links measure 2,936 yards, par 35; the White Links are 3,297, par 36; the new Blue Links are 3,086, par 36. The 150-yard markers are 4 x 4s with yellow numerals. The greens are not lightning fast but not slow either. Except for the occasional gully or mound, the course is built on flat terrain.

The Whites begin with a straightforward par 4 measuring 310 yards. Water sits on the right side near the green. It takes a shameful slice to put a ball in the water, but it happens.

No. 2, a 490-yard par 5, is the number three handicap hole on this nine. A few trees mark the sides of a wide fairway. For straight hitters, this hole won't intimidate. For straight, long hitters though, players who can't resist trying for eagle, there are some problems near the green. The hole has a soft dogleg left. Ahead of the dogleg, on the left side, is a small pond. Bill Payne drove his cart into this water hazard. His feat is immortalized in a cartoon-like poster that stands near the hazard.

No. 3 is a pro-length 440-yard par 4, and it's the number one handicap hole on this nine. (Each of the three nines has handicaps 1 through 9.) Nothing fancy, just straightaway and long. All down the left side, however, are dense underbrush and tall trees, which hide an 8-foot-deep gully. Water courses through the gully, and balls hit into this jungle often stay there, waiting for the sharp-eyed hawker. A large and level green, without hazard, is at the end of the fairway.

Then it's a short walk over a covered bridge to the next tee, shared by a hole from the Red nine. Look before you hit to make sure you don't switch nines by accident. When standing on the tee, it's difficult to see where No. 4 goes. The par 4 is 395 yards and halfway out begins a serious dogleg right. A large sand trap marks the elbow of the dogleg and more sand is on the right of the green. To the left, for players who skipped breakfast for an early tee time, stands a pear tree. At the right time of year, the branches are filled with fruit.

No. 9, a 515-yard par 5, opens straight then turns sharply left near the approach. There, the Bob-O-Link version of the Eisenhower tree sits, a huge cottonwood on the right side of the fairway. In addition, mounds line the right side. On both sides, pines guide to the hole. There is a spot of sand directly in front of the green and a small pond there, as well. The pond cannot be seen until players get close.

On the Red Links, No. 1 is a short par 4, only 317 yards long. There is a little water on the left but it would take a prodigious hook to find it. A pair of traps catch the unwary near the green, which is flat.

On No. 4, a pond sits in front of the tee and should prove to be nothing more than decoration. The hole is a par 4 of 338 yards; 200 yards out is a sharp dogleg left. Fairway traps mark the final few yards to the green and on the left is another small pond, cattails lining its banks.

No. 6 is a 150-yard par 3 that calls for careful club selection; 30 yards in front of the green is water and the green has plenty of sand surrounding it.

No. 8 is a 355-yard par 4,—again there's water in front of the tee. There is also a large trap on the right side of the fairway; to clear it calls for 200-yard carry. Carry, not bounce.

The first two nines are fun to play but have no real signature holes. The third nine, the new Blue Links, is not the longest of the three but is the most interesting. Only 3,086 yards, none of the par 4s on this nine is longer than 375 yards. The two par 5s make up the yardage, measuring 520 and 573. This nine calls for greater golf skills.

No. 1, for instance, is only 320 yards long and could be reached with two mid-iron shots. But no one is likely to pull a mid-iron from their bag on the tee. The hole narrows as it nears the green. Tall hardwoods line the left side of the fairway. Forty yards in front of the green a creek crosses the fairway. With more hardwoods leaning in on the right side, the tee shot and approach shot have to fly true. The greens here are much different from those on the Red and White Links; they are faster and have a great deal of shape to them. Double-break putts are common. If bets are made on this nine, it would pay to bet on the player with the best short game.

Bob-O-Link Golf Course

No. 2 is a par 4 and, at 375 yards, the longest par 4 on this nine. The hole aims left and large mounds mark the right side. The approach must clear a creek 50 yards in front of the green. The green is found at the end of a dogleg right, which begins just past the water.

No. 5, a 520-yard par 5, heads out and to the right over a creek that won't be much trouble, to a small lake that will be. The lake is 150 yards across; once past it, the fairway narrows and cuts right through the forest. The green here is unusual. Narrow and fast, it is almost 50 paces long.

No. 8, the second par 5, is 573 yards and quite rightly designated the number one handicap. The fairway snakes out, bending sharply to the right and then sharply to the left. The canal cuts across the fairway 200 yards before the green, which has sand on the left side.

No. 9 seems to be built as a reward for players shooting par on the last hole. Or a hole to provide solace to those who failed. A par 4, it is only 275 yards from tee to green. In front of the green, however, is the canal. The green has plenty of pitch and roll to it. Just being on in two is no guarantee of par.

Bob-O-Link is a good layout for the average golfer but one that takes a little getting used to. That isn't a fault of the course as much as it is a fact of the terrain. And one of the best things about Bob-O-Link is the number of teenagers playing the course. From a sod farm to a course with a future.

Bob-O-Link Golf Course
4141 Center Rd. (Rte. 83)
Avon, OH 44011   Phone: 835-0676

Manager: Bill Fitch

27 holes

Red & White Tees	Yds.	Course	Slope	Red & Blue Yds.	Course	Slope
Middle:	6233	66.7	105	6022	66.3	111
Back:	n/a	68.1	108	n/a	68.0	115
Forward:	6051	66.6	107	5715	66.7	112

Blue & White Tees	Yds.	Course	Slope
Middle:	6383	67.9	112
Back:	n/a	69.6	115
Forward:	6076	68.4	115

Season:	Mar–Dec
Hours:	6:00 a.m.–10:00 p.m.
Greens fees:	$7.00 / $13.00
Special rates:	seniors & juniors: $4.75 / $9.00
	all day w/ cart: $48.00 for 2 people
Carts:	$7.50 per 9 holes
Tee times:	taken wkends
Practice facilities:	range, putting green, chipping green
Clubhouse facilities:	food, beer, liquor; pavilions
Outings:	regular course events; available for private outings
League play:	various times
Pro shop:	lightly stocked
Lessons:	not available
Ranger:	daily
Special rules:	no coolers on course
New features:	automatic irrigation system on all tees, greens, fairways; 150 trees planted; driving range watered

Boston Hills Country Club
Boston Heights

The course is almost 70 years old—certainly some unusual incidents have occurred here. Riding carts have been driven into the lakes, a helicopter once landed on the fairway in fog, a player was lost to lightning, and, one morning, the starter found a tent filled with campers still sleeping in the 1st fairway.

And Boston Hills made it into Guiness' Book of Records for Charlie Stock's iron man demonstration. It was a fundraising event for the March of Dimes. In 1986, when he played 711 holes in 24 hours, his scorecard showed 82 birdies, more red numbers in one day than many players post in a lifetime. He played 79 nine-hole rounds that day and averaged 36.5 strokes per nine. Par was 35. A bronzed copy of the letter from Guiness acknowledging the feat and its place in the book hangs on a wall in the clubhouse.

Marv Maines is one of the managers of Boston Hills, and he is quick to note the improvements added over the last ten years. "The clubhouse is new. We built it six years ago," he said. "The barn next door is new, about nine or ten years old. We redid the pavilion of the barn. We put on the shelter house."

On a busy day, 300 golfers will play here. During the week, almost 30 leagues provide 900 nine-hole players. Lessons are available from Ron Burke, PGA.

The practice green here is sometimes more difficult than the greens on the course. In addition to the putting green, Boston Hills maintains a practice range. It is one of a number of area courses that stays open, weather allowing, all year. The course was built in 1924 by Wink Chadwick, who ran it as a semi-private course until 1961, when he sold it and the new owners made the course public.

It opens with a comfortably wide par 4, 379 yards from a slightly elevated tee. A small pond sits in front of the tee box and the fairway slopes down all the way to the green; no difficulty getting there. No. 2, which runs parallel to the first hole, rises slightly, but it is only 330 yards yards long. A couple of old hardwoods stand up on the left side of the fairway at about the 100-yard marker. The greens here are very well kept. They are not lightning fast but are quick enough for the average player. At No. 2 green, there is sand on the right and grass bunkers on the left.

No. 3, a 449-yard par 5, is a handsome hole with a blind tee shot. An aiming flag guides players to the optimum landing area. Though it is a decided dogleg right with a huge old maple tree in the elbow of the bend, it's not a particularly challenging par 5, but a beautiful one. On both sides of the wide fairway are hardwoods. The shallow green is egg-shaped and set at an angle. The approach shot here may be the most challenging.

The first par 3, No. 5, is under 100 yards. Many players would score better if they just threw the ball. Between the tee and the green is a tiny lake. The green has old hardwoods on the right and left sides. Bunkers are on both sides, too, and the rear of the green falls steeply away. Only 98 yards, it can be a most confounding hole.

No. 6 is another short hole, a par 4 only 294 yards. It calls for a blind tee shot to a crest marked with an aiming flag. Down the left side, the rough fills with trees. It's hard to see, but the fairway bends sharply off to the left. The green is surrounded with trees and has no sand.

No. 7, a 299-yard par 4, is a straightaway hole with o.b. on the left. A few mounds decorate the fairway but none is problematic. It is followed by another short par 3; No. 8 is 136 yards. The hole is in the corner of the course and runs next to Route 8. Traffic here can be distracting for players on the tee.

No. 9, also in the corner of the course, is a 452-yard par 5 that runs parallel to the road from Route 8 to the clubhouse. It is o.b. on the left side. About 40 yards from the green, there is a small pond well to the right.

The back nine begins with a 336-yard par 4. No. 10 has a blind tee shot to a fairway that rises gently. Once at the crest, the green is visible off to the right, with some sand around it. A few trees guard its right side.

No. 11, a 411-yard par 4, is the number one handicap hole here. A few years ago, it was a par 5. It's another blind tee shot to a very wide fairway that bends sharply to the left. Trees define this hole and prevent cutting the dogleg. The second shot is generally a long one to a small green in a forest of hardwoods.

No. 13, a 461-yard par 5, begins with a tee enclosed in hardwoods and follows aiming flags as the fairway courses down and to the right. Mounds on the right will be cleared by most players' drives. At the green are more mounds on all sides and sand on the right.

No. 15 is a 410-yard par 4 that goes uphill slightly and then bends to the right. It's a wide open hole with mounds and sand traps protecting the green. On the right side of the green is a grass bunker.

The tees and greens are watered here and the fairways fare much better than many when the weather becomes difficult. Recent droughts have not disfigured Boston Hills fairways and pro Ron Burke thinks that it may be due to the age of the course. "I don't know how deep our root system is, but maybe that has something to do with it."

Boston Hills Country Club
105 East Hines Hill
Boston Heights, OH 44236   Phone: 656-2438 Cleve.
                                     650-0934 Akron

Manager: Marv Maines
Pro: Ron Burke, PGA

Tees	Yds.	Course	Slope
Middle:	5769	66.7	107
Back:	6004	67.8	109
Forward:	4991	67.1	104

Season: year-round
Hours: 6 a.m.–7 p.m.
Greens fees: $8.00 / $13.50 wkdays; $9.25 / $17.50 wkends
Special rates: seniors: $9.50 / $15.50 per person (includes riding cart) before 3 p.m. wkdays
                      special discount after 4 p.m. on wkends
Carts: $9.00 / $18.00
Tee times: taken
Practice facilities: driving range, putting green
Clubhouse facilities: snack bar: food, beer, liquor
Outings: two pavilions, up to 250 guests
League play: heavy during week, some on wkends
Pro shop: lightly stocked
Lessons: by appointment
Ranger: daily
New features: cart paths

Brandywine Country Club
Peninsula

"Just the basics," is how Scott Yesberger described the stock in his pro shop. One of the basics is a shirt emblazoned with, "I Survived the Back Nine at Brandywine."

The back side here is legendary, and not just for its Z-hole, the 545-yard par 5 that is almost impossible to eagle. Though it is only 3,032 yards long and has only one par 4 over 400 yards, the back nine, as it twists and turns, rises and falls, calls for a bag filled with a great variety of shots. Approaches from sidehill/uphill lies are not uncommon.

Brandywine's drama is attractive. In the parking lot on a summer day, license plates give indication of the course's drawing power: Cuyahoga, Ashtabula, Stark, Summit, Trumbull, Portage, Huron, and Wayne counties are all there. Peninsula is a very pretty little town and far from the beaten path.

The front side is lovely. It begins with a straightaway 376-yard par 4. The fairway rises and is marked by a century oak on the right side that, though it should not come into play, should stay in players' memories; it is a magnificent old tree. The fairway is generously wide on this hole and the green slopes slightly forward. Sand marks the right edge.

No. 2, a 494-yard par 5, is straight until the last 200 yards, where the hole bends to the right. Trees define the hole both left and right and, on the left, the woods rise steeply. There is enough room on this fairway, though, to make par without much trouble.

On No. 4, a 323-yard par 4, sand, trees, and water combine to make the hole tougher than its length might indicate. The generous fairway takes a sharp left around a lake. The dogleg is marked by sand on either side of the fairway and hickory trees leaning over the water.

No. 8 travels alongside Akron-Peninsula Road as it makes its way back to the clubhouse. This 534-yard par 5 has a wide fairway marked with sand traps on both sides near the 150-yard markers. (Yardage markers are white stakes, easy to spot and recognize.) No. 9 is a par 3 from a tree-canopied elevated tee across a small pond to green with sand on both sides.

The front nine, as noted, is lovely, but the heroic shots and bragging rights come from the back nine. It begins with a 347-yard par 4. From a slightly elevated tee the fairway is straight, though narrow as it nears the green. Woods on either side and an equipment barn on the right emphasize the importance of staying in the fairway. Water comes into play in the last 100 yards, where a creek runs parallel to the fairway. There is sand at the right side of the green.

No. 11 is another par 4, even shorter than No. 10. Though only 301 yards, it calls for some thought at the tee. The fairway twists to the right, then to the left, and then up and right again to the green. It is narrow—at the 150-yard marker only 25 yards across. Two accurate irons will suffice here. The green is raised 8 or 10 feet and is well-protected by sand traps. The creek from the previous hole wanders down the left side.

No. 12 is shorter still, a 277-yard par 4. Cottonwoods and poplars provide shade on the tee; hickories and oaks fill the woods on either side. Again, it's a very narrow fairway. To the left rear of the green, and not visible from the tee, is a lake. The ground behind the green falls away to the water. It's at this hole players realize the game is moving deeper into the hills that previously only lined the fairways.

At No. 13, the fairway dips in front of the tee, then shoots up and veers right. It's a 350-yard dogleg to the right and not one that tempts drivers to clear the elbow. The first couple hundred yards are all up. Yesberger estimates the fairway rises at a 45-degree angle. The turn in the fairway is at the 150-yard marker, after which the fairway dips a few times on its way to the green. On both sides of the fairway, tee to green, mature hardwoods begin where the rough ends. Leaving the narrow fairway at any point can add substantial numbers of strokes. To the right of the green is a large trap.

No. 15 is only 148 yards, but it can be reached with a well-hit short iron; the tee box is virtually the edge of a cliff and the green is 150 feet below. This is one of the signature holes here and is pictured on the scorecard.

Between the 13th tee and the 16th green is the Ohio version of the Khyber Pass. The famous Z-hole—No. 16, a 545-yard par 5 (and number two handicap)—is played on a valley floor. Its fairway goes out straight about 200 yards, takes a sharp right to the 150-yard marker, then an equally sharp left toward a green with sand on the left side. The fairway on this hole is narrow and seems more so because the valley walls rise on both sides. Walking off this green with a 5 is wholly satisfactory.

At 416 yards, No. 17 is the longest par 4 on the course. The hole is defined by rising terrain on the left and a line of firs on the right. It's a big, soft dogleg left with a gently rising fairway.

No. 18 is a 518-yard par 5 that is straight until the last hundred yards, where it sharply turns left to the green. The fairway is wide and rolls gently. Two huge sand traps mark the sides of the fairway around 200 yards from the green. The dogleg has a stand of trees in the elbow that will prevent most big hitters from reaching in two.

On the other side of the road is a par 3 course just created by the Yesberger family on what had previously been a practice area. Brandywine has a juniors program: "We're making a real effort to promote junior golf," Yesberger said. The 1991 season was the first for the juniors, who played in a couple of tournaments, won prizes, and enjoyed an outing at the end of the season. Credit for all the work, Yesberger said, goes to his mother, Lee, and Wendy Mayer. "They did a hell of a job." The program has 65 players.

Yesberger does not know who holds the course record. "I've heard about people shooting 30 on the front nine," he said. What happened to them on the back nine, they didn't say.

Brandywine Country Club
5555 Akron-Peninsula Rd.
Peninsula, OH 44264   Phone: 657-2525

Manager: Scott Yesberger

18 holes
Tees	Yds.	Course	Slope
Middle:	6040	68.4	110
Back:	6580	70.2	113
Forward:	5480	70.5	113

Season:	Mar 15–Dec 1
Hours:	n/a
Greens fees ('91):	$8.00 / $14.00 wkdays; $9.50 / $18.00 wkends
Special rates:	wkdays before 2 p.m.: two players plus cart for $23.00 /$39.00
	seniors: $6.00 / $8.00 Mon–Thu until 2 p.m. And wkends, after 4 p.m.: 9 holes for two players w/riding cart for $25.00
Carts:	$9.00 / $18.00
Tee times:	required wkends, taken wkdays
Practice facilities:	putting green
Clubhouse facilities:	food, beer, liquor; pavilion
Outings:	private outing facilities available
League play:	Mon–Thu afternoons
Pro shop:	lightly stocked
Lessons:	by appointment
Ranger:	wkends
Other:	Junior Golf Program
New features:	18-hole tickets only, wkends until 2 p.m.

Briardale Greens Golf Course
Euclid

The first sign golfers read as they drive into Briardale Greens says, "You play at your own risk here." In the parking lot, the sign reads, "You park at your own risk here." Is there something we should know?

This flat course, managed by Scott Markel, covers almost 250 acres and was designed by area designer and builder Dick LaConte. It was built in 1977. Situated in the middle of this densely populated East Side suburb, it is a very busy course. Tee times are taken for weekday as well as weekend play. A half-dozen or more leagues line up for play on weeknights. The small clubhouse seats only a handful before strangers rub elbows; the well-stocked pro shop is similarly small. For outings, however, the pavilion seats more than a hundred and still has room for grills.

Briardale is not a long course, 5,845 yards, par 70. The fairway is kept at 3/4" and the rough at 2".

No. 1 is a no-frills par 4, 337 yards long. The fairway is defined by a few small stands of trees on both sides and a few bushes. Behind the green is a little lake. No. 2 is a 150-yard par 3. Two substantial traps rest on either side of the green, which is especially handsome for the apron cut in front of it. The apron and the manicuring of the entire course is the work of Wayne Sampson, a soft-spoken greenskeeper who clearly takes pride in his work.

No. 3 is a 350-yard dogleg right around a lake, which is inexplicably marked o.b. Cattails fill the bank on the green side of the water, and there is sand on the left side of the green. The sand slows some balls from bouncing to the chain link fence that marks the edge of the course and the beginning of a residential area.

No. 4, a 370-yard par 4, is a soft dogleg left. There are some trees on the sides of the fairway and several tall, old hardwoods that help narrow the fairway 60 yards from the green. The green is slightly elevated and surrounded by plenty of sand. No. 5, the second of three par 3s on this side, is straightaway and long—190 yards. The green is wide but has sand on the right side and another trap 15 yards in front in the left rough. No. 6 is another straight hole, a par 4 of 410 yards. Along the left side is tall fencing to protect neighbors in their backyards from snap hooks.

The number one handicap hole is next: No. 7, a par 5 of 495 yards, two lakes, tall trees, and a well-bunkered green. In other words, it deserves to be the number one handicap. There are backyards all along the left side and a few trees on the right. About 170 yards from the green, a small lake appears on the right and a second lake behind it. If the lakes don't grab balls sliced from the fairway, tall sycamores on the right side will knock them down. The green has a large trap in front and a smaller trap in the rear.

No. 8 is a 170-yard par 3. Behind the tee is Babbitt Road, from which drivers (of cars) sometimes critique the swings of players. The second body of water on the previous hole shows up on the right side here. Mallards raise families at water's edge. A brace of sand traps rests on the right side of the green.

All of this failed to intimidate Nick Dieglio, Sr. On an August day in 1986 he fired an ace. That is not so rare. But he fired a second ace on No. 11, also 170 yards. According to Golf Digest, only 16 players before Mr. Dieglio managed two aces in the same round. "I was 68 [years old]. I thought the good Lord was trying to tell me something, giving me something before I pass on to another world. But I'm still here," he said late last season. All eyes, of course, were on him when he teed up at No. 16. "And I almost did it," he said. No one, but no one, is on record for firing three aces in the same round. He left it a foot and a half, pin high, from the cup. And then three-putted. "I was putting terrible that day," he said, explaining his 42-42 score. He came close to duplicating the show in August of 1989 when he fired a hole-in-one on No. 2, then hit the flag with his shot on No. 5. He golfs, he said, mostly for the exercise.

No. 9 is a par 5 that faces two small lakes on either side of the fairway. They are decorative, though that doesn't stop a few players every day from hitting balls into them. Down the left side of this 491-yard hole is the entrance road and a few trees. The fairway gets narrow—only 26 yards across at the 200-yard marker. And the green is a small target; there is sand in front, and behind it is a lovely stand of locusts and willows.

The back side starts with another straight par 4. Its 372 yards end at a green with sand on the left front and left rear. All along the left side is the entrance drive. Perhaps it was the this approach that prompted the city to raise all those warning signs.

No. 12 is the only par 5 on the back side, a 470-yard straightaway that looks, because of Wayne Sampson's light mowers on the fairway, as if it were weaved. A creek cuts across the narrow fairway near the green and ties into a lake on the left side. Willows line the right side close to the green, where there is also sand.

No. 13 is a straight par 4, only 305 yards, and parallel to the entrance drive, though on this hole the drive is on the right, so slices are necessary to hit oncoming cars. There are a couple of trees in the fairway. The green slopes forward. No. 15 is a tight par 4, 362 yards, with a thin line of tall hardwoods going down both sides. The trees are especially valuable on the right side, where they protect cars in the parking lot from screaming slices. The fairway is only 23 yards across and the rough on the left side is more rough because of the mounds built there. There is sand on the left at the green and a lake on the right.

No. 17, a wide and straight par 4 of 342 yards, has an elementary school beyond the white stakes on the left side. Sand is in the right rough and also at the green. No. 18 is a 402-

yard par 4 with some trees on the right and a line of young hardwoods growing on the left. About halfway, a pair of traps shows up in the left rough; a huge willow squats on the right side at about 130 yards from the green. There is plenty of sand to prevent rolling the ball onto the green.

Briardale is successful for a short list of reasons. First, location. Setting down an 18-hole layout with a driving range and outing facilities must have been difficult here, but for the thousands of area players who use and enjoy the club, it was an excellent investment. Second, the course is well managed and very well cared for. Finally, the fees charged are minimal and Euclid residents get a break.

Briardale Greens Golf Course
24131 Briardale Ave.
Euclid, OH 44123   Phone: 289-8574

| Manager: | Scott Markel |
| Superintendent: | Wayne Sampson |

Tees	Yds.	Course	Slope
Middle:	5845	68.4	119
Back:	6274	70.5	122
Forward:	5101	68.4	108

Season:	year-round
Hours:	sunrise–sunset
Greens fees:	$7.50 / $12.00 wkdays; $8.50 / $13.00 wknds
Special rates:	seniors: $5.00 / $8.00 wkdays
Carts:	$8.00 / $15.00
Tee times:	taken up to 7 days in advance
Practice facilities:	range, putting green, chipping green, sand trap
Clubhouse facilities:	snack bar: food, beer; pavilion
Outings:	all types available
League play:	Mon–Fri 8:00–10:00 a.m., 3:30–6:00 p.m.
Pro shop:	well stocked
Lessons:	not available
Ranger:	all days
New features:	improving driving range

Briarwood Golf Course
Broadview Heights

Martin Rini, who manages the 27-hole layout at Briarwood, doesn't hesitate when asked his toughest problem.

Geese.

Canada geese. Hundreds and hundreds of the handsome black and gray birds make their home on the lush fairways here. "They chewed up the greens on 13, 14, and 18. And they go for the tender roots, no grubs or anything, just tender grass roots. And goose droppings. On 13, you could not walk across the fairway without stepping on something."

About a hundred of the honkers were captured by state wildlife officials and shipped out, but Rini knows they will be back. In the meantime, the general manager is kept busy with a course on which 32,000 rounds were played last year.

Briarwood is not a historic course, but some golfing greats have played there. The first nine opened in 1966 and the greens fee was $1.50. That was Lochs. A year later, the Glens nine opened. And in 1972, Ben was opened. In 1971, an exhibition match was played between Miller Barber, Bobby Cole, and Jack Nicklaus. Jack lost.

At present, 42 leagues call Briarwood home and the course does a very good trade in outings. The new clubhouse, completed in 1989, seats 160. There is also a pavilion. Adjacent to the course is a driving range where PGA teacher Mike Mural gives lessons. He is highly regarded as both player and teacher and once lost to Gary Player by a mere two strokes. Player remarked at the time that he had never seen a longer hitter than Mural. The score card from the match sits in the trophy case at an East Side private club.

Recent summers, marked by drought, seem to have had little effect on the turf here. There are lakes on the course and fairways are well watered.

The nine holes known as Ben is treated like a kid brother at a neighborhood baseball game, which is to say, tolerated but not admired. That's too bad. Ben is a delightful little nine for a lot of players and if played from the back of the tee boxes, no pushover.

From the whites, it measures 2,765, par 35. Ben has three par 3s and two par 5s. The first par 5 is the opening hole and is 460 yards from tee to green. It has a wide fairway that bends to the left. Down the right side, woods come into play; down the left, hidden from view, is a sizable lake. Before launching the approach shot, players have to watch for other players crossing the fairway—it's the only way to get from the 8th green to the 9th tee.

The rough is playable here and the fairways are lush. The greens are manicured and challenging. No. 2, a par 3 measuring 185 yards, is a good example. From the tee, the left side is deep woods and o.b. The right is open. But the green is given to speed and undulation, so even a good tee shot is no guarantee of par here.

No. 4 is a simple 330-yard par 4, but interesting. It is straight for about 200 yards, then abruptly turns left. Down the left side of the fairway are deep and thick woods, high enough to prevent anyone from cutting the corner. Down the right side, trees guide the player and the terrain drifts off and down. The green has a great deal of action on it. There's a grass bunker in front and deep woods behind.

No. 5 is a 140-yard par 3 with a large green to aim at. Deep woods along the left side shouldn't come into play. No. 6 is a 490-yard par 5 where the drive must carry a narrow lake and climb. The fairway bends slightly and rises slowly but steadily. About a hundred yards from the green, a grass bunker sits in ambush in the right rough. There is no sand here—and very little sand anywhere on the three nines.

No. 7 is a straight par 4, only 265 yards, that dips then rises. It is plenty wide; any difficulty comes from holding the green. No. 8 is the last par 3, a 125-yard hole with mounds on the right side of a sizable green.

Then it's off—across the No. 1 fairway—to the 9th tee. No. 9 is a 380-yard par 4. The tee is elevated and looks down on a lush fairway with only a few potential trouble spots. Lake on the left, another smaller lake on the right. The landing area for tee shots is not generous, though missing the fairway while clearing the water on the right side is not a heavy penalty.

The other two nines, Glen and Lochs, constitute the 18-hole round here. Played from the blue tees, it's a long course: 3,445 yards going out on Glens and 3,540 coming back on Lochs. That's 6,985 yards for a par 72. Even from the white tees, 6,330 yards, it's still fairly long.

No. 1 on Glens is a 360-yard par 4, a suitable warm-up hole that passes a lake on the right of the tee and rises steadily to the green. A few trees down the right side provide guidance; down the left are thick woods.

The No. 2 tee box offers seasonal flowers and a difficult tee shot. The hole, a par 4 that plays 380, starts flat, then drops off to a valley in front of the elevated green. There is water on the right side of the valley. But that's not the difficult part. At about 165 yards from the green in the right side of the fairway is the local Eisenhower tree—actually two shagbark hickories. They effectively cut the width of a fairway that wasn't all that wide to begin with. The rough on the left side is filled with an assortment of trees.

No. 3 is a 505-yard par 5 that is more pretty than difficult. From a slightly elevated tee the first 150 yards are wide open, then the fairway is bordered by trees on either side. Water can come into play as well.

No. 4, a 140-yard par 3, looks easy. The shot is to a large green, but the terrain falls off to the left and the green leans that way as well.

No. 5, a 395-yard par 4, is a blind tee shot into a valley, where players can ring a bell to signal players behind them to shoot. The fairway ambles along peacefully to an elevated green.

No. 6 runs parallel to the previous hole and is a 375-yard par 4. From an elevated tee, the fairway slides down to a valley, then rises sharply and levels at about the 150-yard marker. From there it is straight and wide.

No. 7, a par 5 of 490 yards, has been described by Jim Chorba as one of the best par 5 holes in the area. Chorba is president of the Inter-Club Public Golf Association and has played a lot of par 5s. One hundred yards from the tee the turf drops to a valley. Woods line both sides and are especially heavy on the left. The left side of the fairway rises and falls while the right is reasonably flat. A fast-moving creek crisscrosses the fairway on a diagonal, then lines the right side. At the green, which is elevated, the wide creek runs in front and left. This is the number two handicap hole on this nine.

No. 8, a par 4 of 350 yards, begins from an elevated tee. The fairway drops in front, then begins a long climb up. It lists to port as it rises, and the green is difficult to see.

Making the turn, No. 1 on Lochs is a 360-yard par 4. The wide fairway rises slowly, bottoms out about 50 yards from the green, then rises again. No. 2 is only five yards longer, but this par 4 is far more hazardous. A lake sits in front of the tee. It should not come into play, but it is a distraction. Beyond the lake, trees start on either side and the fairway narrows. About 130 yards from the green, a big crease cuts across the fairway. Ten or fifteen feet deep, the grass-lined gully rises back to the green, which slopes away. With heavy woods behind, it's important to hold this green.

No. 4 is a beautiful par 5. A lake sits in front of the tee box, willows leaning over the far shore on the right side. The lake is only 120 yards across, and when the fairway begins it bends slightly to the left and begins a long, slow rise. A few trees define the hole, and there is pitch and roll to the fairway.

From the 150-yard marker, it falls slightly to a green with no sand.

No. 5 is a 375-yard par 4 that goes out straight until the 150-yard marker. A meddlesome tree sits in the fairway, ten or fifteen yards from the right rough, and strongly encourages tee shots to the left side of the fairway. Just beyond, however, the fairway drops substantially. In the valley is a lake on the right side. The fairway shoots up a steep hill to the green. Two very good shots are called for to get on in regulation.

A split rail fence and well-tended flower garden make the 7th tee especially attractive. It is a rising 365-yard par 4. The green is off to the right and only the top of the flag is visible until the last 100 yards, when the fairway levels. No. 8 is a big par 3. A 190-yard-long valley separates tee from green, though it's open on either side.

No. 9 is another lake hole. This par 4, 400-yard hole rises slightly for the first 200 yards, then drops toward the lake, which is 60 or 70 yards across. There are 40 yards of fairway between lake's edge and the green. The lake grabs plenty of balls, one player noted, because there is a tendency to overhit when clearing it. The downhill lie doesn't help.

Briarwood is a lush course thanks to a multitude of creeks and lakes. The layout successfully exploits the terrain, and the three nines and several tees adapt well to many types of play.

Briarwood Golf Course
2737 Edgerton Rd.
Broadview Hts, OH 44147   Phone: 237-5271

President: Richard Overmyer
General Manager: Martin Rini

27 holes

	Ben & Glen			Lochs & Glen		
Tees	Yds.	Course	Slope	Yds.	Course	Slope
Middle:	5930	68.0	112	6330	69.5	119
Back:	6405	70.2	117	6985	72.8	125
Forward:	5355	69.9	110	5860	71.6	115

	Lochs & Ben		
Tees	Yds.	Course	Slope
Middle:	5930	68.0	111
Back:	6500	70.8	117
Forward:	5365	68.9	108

Season: open from Apr
Hours: sunrise–sunset
Greens fees: $8.75 / $16.00 wkdays; $9.50 / $18.00 wkends
Special rates: none
Carts: $9.00 / $18.00
Tee times: taken wkends & holidays
Practice facilities: range, putting green
Clubhouse facilities: snack bar: food, beer, liquor; banquet rooms
Outings: available
League play: wkdays
Pro shop: well-stocked
Lessons: by arrangement
Ranger: wkends & evenings
Special rules: no tank tops

Brunswick Hills Golf Course
(a.k.a. Bramblewood)
Brunswick

Twenty-five years ago, a group of golfers pooled their loot, bought this farmland, and ordered built the first nine holes of Brunswick Hills. It is an easy front nine, with generous fairways and level ground. The stockholders built most of the second nine themselves. What a difference. It's a hilly, beautiful romp through woods of hawthorn, ash, maple, cottonwood, and pines.

JoAnne Welling manages the course. She provides all the fixings for outings, helps gets leagues off on time, maintains a small pro shop and brags, "We treat everybody like family here." League play is scheduled every day of the week but is not heavy.

The clubhouse seats 49 without crowding. In front of the one-story clubhouse is a putting green, but the course has neither staff professional nor driving range. At 6,391 yards, par 72, Brunswick Hills is one of the longer courses in the area. It stays open year-round.

Play begins on a 355-yard par 4 across a valley to a wide and trouble-free fairway. The valley, which cuts across the fairway, has a stream coursing through it and will affect play on holes 5, 7, and 9, too. On the back side, the stream will influence play on more than half the holes. The first green is slightly elevated but has no sand.

No. 3, a 347-yard par 4, plays along the southern border of the course. The right side is o.b., but the left side has only a few pine trees. Missing the fairway with a hook doesn't mean giving up on par.

No. 5 begins and ends with water. To get to the tee, players walk past a large pond. At the tee, they turn around and hit over it. It is a long par 4, 441 yards, and the number two handicap hole. The wide fairway rises beyond the water. The green is elevated five or six feet; behind it is a lake. That lake turns into a hazard from the next tee. No. 6 is a dogleg right and the first part of the hole has the lake on the right side. It plays 387 yards and it's not really fair to cut the corner of the dogleg. It is also marked o.b., to protect players on a tee there.

No. 7, a 398-yard par 4, begins with a blind tee shot down a fairway that rises slightly, crests, and drops into a watery valley at about the 150-yard marker. The fairway climbs out of this valley and rises to a pretty green with a stand of pines behind it. It's a bit of a walk to get to No. 8, a very long 216-yard par 3. Regulars here play an extra club because it often plays into a headwind.

The front nine is fun, wide open, and not difficult. The back nine is fun, tight, and tough.

Players lulled by the front side are brought up short with No. 10, a big dogleg to the left of 355 yards. Attempts to cut the corner are thwarted by a stand of tall trees. Along the right side, the course property ends and o.b. begins. And the sloped green is not easy to hold.

No. 12, a 399-yard par 4, is a beautiful hole. What appears to be a tree farm bounds the right side, and a couple of stands of trees on the left make this fairway narrow. It is not only narrow, but fast headed downhill, where it crosses a creek then rises to a lovely green balanced on the side of a hill.

Holes No. 12 through 15 play parallel; each has hills and water. No. 13 continues the physical beauty of the back nine. It is a par 4, 383 yards, played in deep woods. From an elevated tee, players look out across a tree-lined valley and the creek that cuts through it. Some extra thought must go into this tee shot if a level stance is desired for the approach. Hitting over the water is not difficult; neither is it difficult to hit in front of the water (hitting *into* the water, of course, is a breeze.) But there is little flat ground on either side. Once over the water, the fairway rises to the green.

Brunswick Hills Golf Course

No. 14, a 325-yard par 4, continues the roller coaster ride. Missing the fairway can prove costly, but even being on the fairway, with its uneven lies, calls for concentration. This is clearly a side that favors experience.

No. 15, a long, 568-yard par 5, has all the virtues and beauty of the last three holes—in spades. Not only does the creek have to be cleared, it has be watched, too. After crossing the fairway, it sneaks up the right side. The fairway narrows in the last 200 yards. It ends at a small green; three very good shots are needed to reach it in regulation.

The ride is not quite finished: No. 16 starts at another elevated tee overlooking the valley. The hole is a 385-yard par 4 and the tee shot here can be intimidating; trees on both sides and an up-and-down fairway make the target area small.

A pleasant walk through the woods leads to the next tee. No. 17 is a par 3 and, only 124 yards, a bit of a relief. The finishing hole is another par 5, this one 501 yards. The fairway, in addition to rising and falling, bends to the right. There is no sand at the green (as there is virtually none on the back side).

The shareholders who designed this back nine just followed Mother Nature and let her have her way. There is nothing forced or artificial about the holes; each takes advantage of the terrain. So there are holes that are both esthetically pleasing and very challenging.

Changes are being made, improvements and additions developed here. It's a remarkable little course and one not as well known as it should be.

Brunswick Hills Golf Course
4900 Center Rd. (Rte. 303)
Brunswick, OH 44212   Phone: 225-7370

Manager: JoAnne Welling

Tees	Yds.	Course	Slope
Middle:	6391	70.3	n/r
Back:	6581	71.1	n/r
Forward:	4823	74.1	n/r

Season: year-round
Hours: 5:30 a.m.–10 p.m.
Greens fees: $7.50 / $14.00 wkdays; $8.50 / $15.00 wkends
Special rates: seniors (over 60) and juniors (under 17): $4.00 / $7.00 wkdays before 3 p.m. Senior cart rate: $7.00 / $14.00 wkdays before 3 p.m.
Carts: $9.00 / $17.00
Tee times: taken wkends
Practice facilities: putting green
Clubhouse facilities: snack bar: food, beer, liquor
Outings: seating for 120
League play: wkdays
Pro shop: lightly stocked
Lessons: not available
Ranger: wkends, holidays, and during league play
New features: new cart paths on front nine; construction of cart paths continues on back nine; 70 Scotch and white pines newly planted

Bunker Hill Golf Course
Medina

Arnold Ingraham's faith in mankind took a brutal hit a few years ago. A foursome teed off at his course and made its way to the first green. Once there, one player suddenly clutched his chest and keeled over from a heart attack. Other members of the foursome tried to revive him, a task made more difficult by the foursome behind yelling and insisting that CPR only held up the game. Get the body—dead or alive—off the putting green, they yelled.

Ingraham's family has had Bunker Hill for about 50 years, and Ingraham left corporate legal work to assume the manager's post about a decade ago.

This hilly and pretty 18-hole layout on Pearl Road, just a bit north of Medina Town Square, is the oldest course in the county, Ingraham said. (Skyland Golf Course in Hinckley also vies for the title.) The first nine holes were laid out in 1927. About 35 years later, the back nine was added.

"It was built as courses were built in those days," Ingraham said. "Particularly the front, where the greens are small. And there are a lot of bunkers—not sand bunkers, but hill bunkers. We're getting back to some of the more traditional types of hazards. It may be a trend now for several reasons. One is that the maintenance cost is much lower. Also, if you look at St. Andrews and the traditional courses—that's what they have."

It's a nice clubhouse with a porch overlooking the first tee. The pro shop is limited. Leagues play all week in the afternoons and early evenings. Tee times are a good idea on weekends but are not taken during the week. A large picnic pavilion is far enough from the course that the yelling and laughing that attend outings won't bother players on the course. Volleyball and bocci are regular features at outings here.

From the first tee, No. 1 fairway drops to a valley, then shoots back up. It's quite wide as the fairway levels out and proceeds to the small green. There are grass and sand bunkers on this 340-yard par 4. No. 2 (which features a beautiful flower garden at the tee) and No. 3 (which plays along the outside edge of the course grounds) are both short par 4s. Trouble lurks, however, for the approach shot on No. 3. The green slopes, and if the shot misses left, the ball is likely to be swallowed by nearby dense underbrush.

No. 5, a par 5 of 480 yards, is a challenging layout. It bends sharply to the left and tempts drivers to cut the corner; hazards include sand on the right side of the fairway and a stream hidden by trees to the right of the green. The fairway is narrow and even prudent players must concentrate to par this hole.

No. 8, a short par 4 whose tee box is almost in a neighbor's yard, is a blind tee shot through a narrow gap in trees. The trees do not really hinder the drive but do remind players of the importance of lining up properly. The fairway rises; even at the 150-yard marker only the top of the flagstick is visible. Five big old pines stand at the right rear of the green, one of the smallest on the course.

No. 9 is another hole that has drama without length. It's only 300 yards from tee to green—some players might reach with a pair of 7 irons. The tee is elevated and the fairway slides down and narrows. Trees fill both sides. The fairway then rises to an elevated green. Before the green, however, is a creek which snares a remarkable number of balls. The local rule here is interesting: "Ladies—if drive comes to rest in second creek on #9—free drop at point of entry." Oh, chivalry!

There is another noteworthy rule posted on the scorecard and it includes all players: winter rules are in effect year 'round. That can confuse players because winter rules are inexact at best. Some people think it means lifting and cleaning a ball at anytime during a match, others think improving a lie in the rough is permissible.

No. 10 is a 564-yard par 5. It runs parallel to No. 1 and has the same valley in front of the tee. Once that valley is carried, it's an open path to the green. There is water on the right side that only a severe slice would reach. For golfers who see every par 5 as a birdie opportunity, bad news: this is the only par 5 on this side.

No. 12 is a long par 3, 188 yards to a green that plays smaller for the trees crowding on both sides. Not visible from the tee is a small pond on the right rear of the green. It is reachable by over-hitters.

No. 16 is one of the signature holes here, an unusually short par 4. Drives are made from a high tee; the fairway begins in the deep valley in front. A creek ambles along the left side and a pond sits on the right side. At the green, a huge guardian tree closes down the right. This is one of many holes here that call for golf skills other than the ability to hit a long ball.

The last three holes are not long, but they can provide an adventurous finish to the round. No. 16 is a short par 4, only a tempting 278 yards from an elevated tee. But with a pond on the right and a creek on the left, accuracy is more valuable than length. No. 17 is a short par 3 of 134 yards, but to a green almost 20 feet higher than the tee and well protected on the right front by an old ash. No. 18 is a 379-yard par 4. The fairway is narrow, the landing area not generous. The approach has to cover water; two creeks cross before the green.

The course plays 5,737 yards, par 70, so it is not long. But it does call for a range of skills and rewards consistent play. Arnold Ingraham enjoys the customers he has today and makes plans for the customers of tomorrow. Like many owners, he has a junior program; on Friday mornings, 60 to 80 kids will show up for instruction and play. "All courses should have a junior league," he said, "but most don't want to bother with it because it's a hassle at times." Ingraham is a gentleman of golf. He runs an antique course and introduces the game to the next generation.

Bunker Hill Golf Course
3060 Pearl Rd.
Medina, OH 44256   Phone: 722-4174

Manager: Arnold Ingraham

18 holes
Tees   Yds.   Course   Slope
Middle: 5737   67.1   107
Forward: 5141   68.9   110
Back: 6044   n/r   n/r

Season: Mar–Nov
Hours: 7:00 a.m.–10:00 p.m. wkdays
                      sunrise–sunset wkends
Greens fees: $8.50 / $16.50
Special rates: senior & junior rates, wkday specials
Carts: $8.50 per 9 holes
Tee times: taken wkends & holidays
Practice facilities: putting green
Clubhouse facilities: snack bar: food, beer, liquor; locker rooms
Outings: large pavilion for special events
League play: wkday evenings & some mornings
Pro shop: lightly stocked
Lessons: not available
Ranger: wkends & holidays
New features: lengthening some tees; starting fairway irrigation

Chardon Lakes Golf Course
Chardon

This tough and pretty course opened in 1931. It has a wonderful history marked with great names: Tom Weiskopf, Jack Nicklaus, and Arnold Palmer have gone around here more than once. Weiskopf's parents were members throughout the sixties. And Nicklaus holds the course record, a 67 shot during an American Cancer Society benefit in 1974.

The course has seen the occasional disaster, too, as builder and resident pro Don Tincher said. Once, two friends were playing on a foggy day, playing the same brand, type, and number of golf ball. On a par 3, both fired into the heavy mist toward the hole. When they arrived at the green, they discovered one ball in the cup, the other within a few feet. Someone fired an ace, but we'll never know who.

A big, comfortable clubhouse with a good kitchen tempts players to stop at the turn for more than a soft drink or beer. Within the same large room is a more-than-adequate pro shop.

There are practice green and driving range, and lessons available from Mike Martin, PGA. Tincher keeps the fairway trimmed to a tight 1/2" and the greens at a very quick 3/16". Like Weiskopf's parents, anyone can become a member here; season memberships are available.

Par is 72 over 6,174 yards. Out-of-bounds appears on the first five holes and again on the back side. Aprons in front of the green add a country club touch to the course. Another such touch is yardage marked on sprinkler heads. The 150-yard markers are Norway spruces.

No. 1 is a 348-yard par 4 that begins at a tee with a sign reading: "No Mulligans." No hitting 'til you're happy here.

The hole bends softly to the left and a line of pines runs down the right side. There are a few trees on the left, but it is not a tight fairway. The first green has sand on both sides and is filled with subtle undulation. The following seventeen greens are of the same style.

No. 2 is the only par 5 on the front side and is a short 473 yards. A lake on the right side of the tee should not come into play. Pines are on both sides of the fairway and on the right is a housing development. A big slice can put the ball into a sunroom. The straight fairway rises gradually to a green with sand on the right front.

No. 4 is a long 205-yard par 3 uphill all the way. On the right, o.b. leads into a field with a sign promising "You'll be Prosecuted to the Fullest Extent of the Law" for trespassing. Sounds like looking for a ball is a felony. A rude touch to a game marked by civility.

No. 5 is a 413-yard par 4 from a slightly elevated tee. The hole is open, with just a few trees on either side. The fairway bends slightly to the right. In the elbow is sand, and there is sand again at the green, where two big traps dominate the left side and one huge trap, the right. Behind the green is a forest of tall pines.

No. 6 is a beautiful hole. An old stone stairway leads up to the blue tees. The hole leaves straight from the tee then turns sharply left toward the green. This 384-yard par 4 has plenty of creek defining the right side. For the last stretch into the green, pines mark the left side and water marks the right. It's a very narrow fairway coming in, only 18 yards across. Little wonder this is the number one handicap hole.

No. 9 tee box has an intercom for players wishing to place orders with the clubhouse kitchen. This is a 386-yard par four that is pinched halfway to the green and marked with sand traps on both sides. Traps are on both sides of the green as well.

The first of two par 5s on the back side is No. 12—short at 471 yards. A wall of pines fills the left side. On the right is o.b.

A creek cuts across the fairway at the forward tees then continues down the left. The hole has a soft dogleg right, and the fairway rises near the green. Sand in the fairway as well as at the green provide hazards here.

No. 13, a 362-yard par 4, bends around to the left. A scenic little lake right in front of the tee adds ambience. More sand on this hole at the 150-yard markers, as well as on both sides of the green.

No. 14 is a magnificent par 3 with a slightly elevated tee. It is 205 yards to a big pitched green with sand on the right front and left side. No. 15 is a 356-yard par 4 with pines going down both side of the hole and the trademark two sand traps on both sides of the green.

No. 16 is a sharp dogleg left. The 382-yard par 4 has pines along the right side, and after turning the corner players see a creek crossing the fairway about 60 yards from the green. Sand and mounds protect this green in the front. It falls off sharply on the left side toward a small creekbed. This is the number two handicap hole.

No. 17 is a 518-yard par 5 with creek cutting across the fairway about 100 yards from the green. On the right near the green is a pond that has swallowed thousands of sliced balls. Getting to the green should be a simple matter. It's a wide fairway here with a few stands of trees on either side. But the water combines with elevated green, large trap on the right, and small one on the left, make finishing the hole difficult.

Chardon Lakes is a challenging golf course in good hands. Shooting for a record held by Nicklaus adds glamour.

Chardon Lakes Golf Course
470 South St.
Chardon, OH 44024   Phone: 285-4653

Manager: Michael Martin

18 holes
Tees   Yds.   Course   Slope
Middle: 6174   70.2   129
Back: 6780   73.1   135
Forward: 5685   66.6   111

Season: Mar 15–Nov 15
Hours: 7:00 a.m.–9:00 p.m.
Greens fees: $15.00 wkdays; $20.00 wkends
Special rates: senior special; season pass available
Carts: $18.00
Tee times: advised, not required
Practice facilities: range, putting green
Clubhouse facilities: food, beer, liquor; private pavilion
Outings: booked by availability
League play: various times
Pro shop: well stocked
Lessons: $15.00 to $25.00 / hr.; by appointment
Ranger: yes
Special rules: carts required before noon on wkends & holidays; no-smoking clubhouse

Cherokee Hills Golf Club
Valley City

An old and handsome red barn has served as clubhouse at Cherokee Hills for many years. Ed Haddad owns the 30-year-old course and hopes to expand the facility to include a party center, larger parking lot, and new clubhouse. He has great plans for improving and expanding the layout itself, too, on which his personal best is a 68.

In the meantime, he runs an interesting and very challenging golf course. And it is open for play—weather permitting—all year. George Jay, manager, said, "I don't ever remember opening or closing." They play the game at a quick pace here; at the third tee, for example, a sign reads: "If it has taken you more than 25 minutes to get here, you are playing too slowly."

Tee times are taken for weekend play; the rest of the week is open. A dozen leagues play here regularly and outings are often held on weekends. About 30,000 rounds are played annually. Though this is not a particularly long course—6,010 yards, par 69 (only one par 5 on each side)—it offers some tough holes.

The opener, a 340-yard par 4, starts at an elevated tee. It's a lovely view, one of the higher spots on the course. The fairway looks like a big emerald carpet unrolled toward the green. It is lined on both sides with trees. Closer to the green, a creek shows up on the left side in the rough, and a huge old willow stands at the left side of the green. There is sand in the back.

At No. 3, a flower box brightens the tee and softens the cautioning language of the "play faster" sign. It is a 390-yard par 4, a dogleg to the right. Beech and ash trees line the right side and a lake sits to the right of the rough near the 150-yard marker.

No. 5, a 390-yard par 4, is played in a shallow valley. Fifty yards in front of the green is the lake, another 50 yards in length. It is more of a psychological hazard than anything else, though a ball hit into it will call not for therapy but stroke and distance. The hole is open except for the area near the green, where trees lean in and demand more of the approach shot. A beautiful, rolling green begins at fairway level then weaves, bobs, and rises. It is longer than it is wide. Getting on in regulation may be the easy part.

That challenging hole is good practice for No. 6, a 510-yard par 5 played on ground high and low, wide and very narrow, and including a huge sycamore stuck right in the middle of the fairway. From the tee, the hole begins innocently enough by stretching straight out for 250 yards. A lake appears on the right side but should not come into play. The surprise is on the left, where the fairway falls over and down a steep hill and then shoots off to the right. In the middle of this low ground is the sycamore. Behind it a hundred yards or so is the green, stuck in the base of a hill. Making matters more interesting is a creek down the left side of the last part of the fairway that then cuts across in front of the green. This hole can likely be played a dozen different ways, and scoring well on it has to be a matter of experience with the hole as well as excellent shotmaking.

After playing The Hole From Another Planet, No. 7, a 320-yard par 4, will be a relief. The fairway, mostly open, bends only slightly right. Another sign at the tee box here nags slow players: "If it has taken you more than 95 minutes to get here, you are playing too slowly." On the right side at the 150-yard marker is a stand of trees and beyond the trees a small pond not visible until players reach it. The fairway rolls to this green, which has a high-lipped sand trap in the right front.

No. 9 is a 375-yard par 4. The tee box is shaded by sycamore and hickory trees and the fairway is quite narrow for the first hundred yards. The fairway rises slightly and at the crest provides players with a splendid view of the clubhouse/barn as well as the green in the distance.

No. 10 is a 410-yard par 4, a hole with generous fairway and water at the green. It finishes at the low point on the course and getting back out and up to the next tee can wind players not used to hauling their own clubs over hill and dale.

No. 12 is a par 3, a beautiful hole of 160 yards—many of them watery. A large lake dominates the right side; the water reaches and partially surrounds the green. Better in the drink, though, than bouncing across Route 303, which runs down the right side of this hole.

A stepladder on the tee is a good indication that the shot will be blind. So it is at No. 13, where a 390-yard par 4 rolls and rises to the 150-yard marker before heading downhill. Sand is on both sides of the green and, more dangerous, a good-sized lake rests on the left.

No. 14, the number one handicap, is a 420-yard par 4 that calls for accurate shots to a green filled with surprises. One hundred yards in front of the tee, the fairway drops to a creek cutting across then starts rising again. Hardwoods line both sides as the fairway crests about 180 yards from the green. An ancient white oak stands on the right side there. The fairway continues to dip and rise, but it runs straight to the green, which has trees around it and unseen tricky breaks underneath it.

No. 15 gets a little tougher. It is a narrow, 390-yard par 4 that runs along the edge of the property. Fades insignificant on other tees will be lost balls on this one.

No. 18 is the only par 5 on this side, a 510-yard hole that plays along in a valley. The left side of the fairway rises steeply. About 200 yards out, a creek cuts across the fairway then runs down the right side to the green. There is no sand at the level green, which is one of the biggest on the course—38 yards across.

Cherokee Hills offers a layout that provides for a few holes of Adventure Golf and should not be missed.

Cherokee Hills Golf Club
5740 Center Rd. (Rte. 303)
Valley City, OH 44280   Phone: 225-6122

Owner: Ed Haddad
Manager: George Jay

18 holes
Tees   Yds.   Course   Slope
Middle: 6010   n/r   n/r
Forward: 5130   n/r   n/r

Season: year-round
Hours: sunrise–sunset
Greens fees: $7.50 / $13.50 wkdays; $8.50 / $15.00 wkends
Special rates: various—call for details
Carts: $8.00 / $16.00
Tee times: taken, not required
Practice facilities: putting green, chipping green
Clubhouse facilities: food, beer, liquor; private rooms
Outings: regular course events; private outings available
League play: various times
Pro shop: well stocked
Lessons: not available
Ranger: daily

Creekwood Golf Club
Columbia Station

The pro at Creekwood Golf Club is a dead dog. Sally Sandvick, manager of the course, explained that Harry Parker, PGA, holder of the course record, "begged for hot dogs, but he didn't chase golf balls," as if you could expect that in a pro.

Turns out that Sandvick's parents, who built the course, found a puppy in a ditch near the course and took him home. The pup went to work every day with them and answered when they called him Harry Parker—the name came from a race horse, a trotter. The dog's picture is on the mantel in the small clubhouse. When local papers called each spring to put their golf lists together, Harry was listed as pro. It was an inside joke to the regulars at Creekwood.

It is not likely that Joe Gawel, retired truck driver, will be as well-known as Harry, but with two aces within one week in 1991, he comes close. He plays Creekwood regularly and was familiar with the 175-yard No. 4 and 155-yard No. 7. He explained his golfing prowess as, "Luck, luck, luck," and said it felt "Great, great, great." He added that the difficulty now is, "You get the idea you can do it again."

It was Sally Sandvick's father, David Sandvick, who built the course, which plays 6,117, for par of 72. There are no blue tees here and winter rules apply year-round. A bricklayer who loved the game, Sandvick needed three years to build the front nine, which opened in 1960. Six years later, the back side was completed. Sandvick died in 1967 and succeeding management of the course was not was it should have been.

"It was a cow pasture," Ms. Sandvick said. "It was the place everyone came when they couldn't get off anyplace else. No leagues, no outings." From that dismal situation, the rebuilding of the course and restoration of its reputation was a formidable task. The Sandvick family has been at it ten years. It looks like it. The course is in good shape; the drainage problem of years ago grows smaller every year. "My brother lays a mile of tile every season," Sandvick said. Tees and greens are watered. The grass is kept to 1" in the fairway, 2" in the rough, and 5/32" on the greens.

The first hole is wide open and long, a 430-yard par 4. Water is on the right as one nears the green, but it should not be a problem. Sand is used judiciously here and seems to be of a finer grain than that of other clubs. This is a good warm-up hole with a green that is easily chipped to.

The No. 2 hole is a 335-yard par 4 with stands of hickory and oak on either side. A creek cuts across the fairway. A cautious player, studying the tall hardwoods on either side, might opt for an iron from this tee.

No. 3 is another short par 4, only 330 yards. It has an attractive tee backed up by old hardwoods. Again, trees line both sides, and about 180 yards out the local version of the Eisenhower Tree threatens even balls hit to the fairway. A pretty pond sits next to the green; a big oak provides shade for the water.

The first of the par 5s is No. 5, a straightaway 507 yards. The left side of the rough leads to o.b., but the hole is a simple one. No. 6, a 360-yard par 4, calls for two irons or a carry from the tee of 190 yards over water. No. 9 is another simple par 5, a wide open 515 yards.

Several of the greens have steep sides to them; missing the green and hitting the side can send a ball 30 or 40 yards.

No. 10 is an interesting hole, not only because it is a 365-yard par 4 with a difficult dogleg in it, but because Sally Sandvick tells a funny story about it. A man brought his wife to the club and proceeded to teach her the game. At the 10th hole, she got too close to his swing and the resulting blow knocked her cold. Terribly shaken, the man revived her, took her to the clubhouse where he secured a sack of ice for her head, and insisted that she relax. While he finished his round.

While No. 10 appears wide open, the 365-yard dogleg to the left calls for some accuracy off the tee. The elbow of the dogleg, which veers to the left, is filled with tall hardwoods and sits on the edge of a creek running across the fairway. It is here that the women's tee is placed, one of the few women's tees on this course that looks like it was not designed as an afterthought. Going down the right side of the fairway is o.b. A rail fence marks the end of the course property, and the farm there—fields, silo, barn—is beautiful.

Holes 13, 14, and 15 constitute Amen Corner as designed by Bizzarro. No. 13 is a 330-yard par 4. One fifty out and then 150 to the left is a suspiciously short 330 yards. The trouble is the corner of the dogleg; it holds the next tee, and players trying to cut the corner run the risk of killing someone on the tee. White stakes make the area out of bounds.

No. 14 is 315-yard par 4. It is straightaway and a good birdie opportunity. No. 15 is a 455-yard par 5 that is straight until the final 50 yards, at which point the fairway lurches to the right. In the elbow of the tight dogleg is a stand of tall hardwoods. To get on in two calls for a shot not found in most bags: a high, long fade that drops suddenly. And while chipping the last shot to the green, one runs the risk of getting clobbered by players on the 13th tee. A very crowded corner, it would be a good place for a full-time course ranger.

The final holes play on more open territory. No. 16 is a 395-yard par 4 that begins at a snug little tee and then opens dramatically. The hole is a dogleg left with some water on the left of the green. No. 17 is a short par 3 with a most impressive tee box. It sits in front of water and is shaded by three huge old willows. The finishing hole is only 315 yards, a par 4 with no surprises.

Creekwood is a wonderful neighborhood course. The men and women who call it their home course are loyal because of the service provided by the Sandvick family. "If you come out a few times, and we get familiar with you," Sally Sandvick said, "then you meet everyone else." It is a friendly game played here.

Players who don't want to pay greens fees every round can pay an annual fee for unlimited golf (and the course is open year 'round.) Senior golfers can enjoy the same benefits for a discounted price.

Creekwood Golf Club
2286 North Reed Rd.
Columbia Station, OH 44028   Phone: 780-1312 Cleve.
                                       748-3188

Owners: Sally & Dale Sandvick
                   June Raymond

18 holes

Tees	Yds.	Course	Slope
Middle:	6117	n/r	n/r
Forward:	4775	n/r	n/r

Season: year-round
Hours: sunrise–sunset
Greens fees ('91): $6.00 / $11.25 wkdays; $6.50 / $12.00 wknds
Special rates: seniors: $4.00 / $7.00
                     2 players w/cart, 18 holes: $25.00 (seniors: $22.00)
                     memberships, gift certificates available
Carts: $8.00 / $15.00; (seniors: $6.50 / $13.00)
Tee times: required wkends & holidays
Practice facilities: range, putting green
Clubhouse facilities: food, beer
Outings: course outings, private outings available
League play: various times—openings available
Pro shop: lightly stocked
Lessons: not available
Ranger: daily during peak season

Deer Track Golf Club
Elyria

Deer Track is a course that grew up. It started as a par 3 and driving range in 1958. In 1970, it was turned into an executive length, nine-hole layout. In 1972, Tony Dulio, PGA, and his late father, Jim, bought the place and remodeled it, making a regulation par 36. The second nine opened in July of 1989. The course name was originally Midway; it was renamed when the back nine was built. Inspiration for the new name came from the deer tracks that filled the newly cleared land.

Though Dulio remodeled the front side and designed the back, he has yet to play a round of golf here. Oh, he's played the front side and he's played the back, but he's never played 18 holes together. "Too busy," he explained. Before joining his father (a construction worker and musician), Dulio attended Michigan State University, where he studied golf club management. Even with 20 years under his belt, he can still be surprised. When he had a dredging company come out to rake lost balls from the water hazards, more than 12,000 were retrieved. "Unbelievable," he said. "Never expected that." And somewhere in a field adjoining the back nine lives a red fox with his own hoard of balls. He takes them from greens before players get there. Dulio's theory is simple: "He thinks they're eggs, and there must be a pile of golf balls in that fox's den." Players have complained of the fox, sitting near the green until an approach shot lands on it, then snatching the ball and fleeing to high grass. "Funny as hell," Dulio said.

Almost 25,000 rounds are played here every season, which begins in March and ends in November or December, depending on weather. Outings are popular, thanks to a pavilion that seats 150 and to the services of a caterer. Plans for the near future call for irrigating the fairways. At present, tees, greens, and a few fairways are watered.

The course begins with a short and straight par 4 of 305 yards. A warm-up hole. The only trouble might come from overhitting the approach shot and landing in the water behind the green. No. 2 is a 371-yard dogleg to the left, a par 4 that calls for an accurate drive and a more accurate second shot. The greens here are beautiful, all well cared for and challenging. At this green, sand lies on both sides. The use of man-made lakes and mounds adds a great deal to an otherwise flat layout.

The only par 5 on the front side is No. 4; it measures 515 yards and bends softly to the left. For the last hundred yards or so, trees in the rough make the fairway narrow. More sand rests on the right side of the fairway.

The green on the par 3 No. 5 is a long 195 yards from the tee. Though generous in size, it has plenty of mystery under the grass. Here's a chance to prove one's green-reading talents. It slopes forward, is slightly elevated, and falls off on the sides and rear.

No. 6 is a short par 4, only 344 yards, but is one of the holes that Dulio considers especially challenging. From the tee box, the fairway shoots out a hundred yards and then bends to the right. On the left is o.b. and deep underbrush. For players who can nail a soft fade off the tee, this is a perfect opportunity. But the landing area is narrow, and blocking the view from the tee down the right side is a huge mound at the bend in the fairway. Aiming over the mound is the best shot here. The next surprise is the lake in front of the green. Players getting on in two here must have confidence in their shotmaking.

No. 8 is the number one handicap hole, a very difficult dogleg left. It calls for a minor tee shot but an approach of heroic proportions. It is 398 yards, though no one wants to play it down the center of the fairway. Dulio said that the tee shot can call for a drive anywhere from 180 to 230 yards, depend-

Deer Track Golf Club

ing on location of the tee. There is a long and narrow lake along the left side of the fairway from the tee. After less than 200 yards, the fairway abruptly turns left. From the tee, players look down a fairway with tall trees on both sides. These narrow the fairway considerably. So it's a tough—some might call it confusing—tee shot. The second shot has to be a long iron or fairway wood down a narrow fairway. Behind the green is plenty of water.

No. 10 begins the tougher of the two sides, though this is not the hole with which to make that argument; it's a straightaway par 4 of 377 yards. The fun begins on No. 11, a narrow par 4 of 357 yards. The hole aims left and, about a hundred yards or so out, it bends back to the right. At the dogleg is a long mound that runs for about 50 yards. Tall hardwoods line both sides of the fairway. Water shows up at the left front of the green and it curls around that side to the rear. There are three traps on the right, and the green itself slopes steeply left.

No. 14 is a short 289-yard par 4. Trees on the left and right are a bright and rich green from spring through summer. And in fall, the maples and sweetgums assume Nature's deepest and most beautiful hues. For players interested more in beach than arbor, there is plenty of sand on this hole—both fairway traps and bunkers at the green. The green is relatively large and given to swells that can quickly add three strokes to the score.

No. 15, a 525-yard par 5, has o.b. down the left side while the hole itself bends a bit to the right. It takes three shots to get to this green and the approach shot has to clear substantial water in front of the green.

No. 16 is a soft dogleg to the left, a 371-yard par 4 with water in front of the green. It is reasonably open on the right side, but the left is fraught with trouble. First, very tough rough. Then the white stakes begin—the green is stuffed into the corner of the course. The wide trap across the front of the green means no bouncing it on.

Like a lot of courses, Deer Track is played better with experience. It's a good-looking course that also looks very young. And as it matures, the play will become better. Tony Dulio seems committed to that.

Deer Track Golf Club
9488 Leavitt Rd.
Elyria, OH 44035   Phone: 986-5881

Owner, Pro:	Tony Dulio, PGA		
18 holes			
Tees	Yds.	Course	Slope
Middle:	6159	69.0	121
Back:	6410	70.1	123
Forward:	5191	68.6	113

Season:	year-round
Hours:	8:00 a.m.–4:00 p.m. Jan–Mar
	6:00 a.m.–10:00 p.m. Apr–Oct
	8:00 a.m.–4:00 p.m. Nov–Dec
Greens fees:	$6.25 / $11.50 wkdays; $6.50 / $12.50 wkends & holidays
Special rates:	seniors: $4.00 per 9 holes, $14.00 per 18 w/ cart
Carts:	$8.50 / $17.00
Tee times:	taken, not required
Practice facilities:	range, putting green, chipping & bunker green
Clubhouse facilities:	snack bar: food, beer, liquor
Outings:	pavilion for regular course events & outside outings
League play:	various times
Pro shop:	well stocked
Lessons:	$20.00 per 1/2 hr., Mon–Fri 1:00–3:00 p.m.
Ranger:	occasional
Special rules:	no coolers or alcohol on course
New features:	women's tees enlarged & watered; fairway watering system started; target greens on range; practice green & bunkers

Dorlon Park Golf Course
Columbia Station

Stacy Johnson, the course superintendent at this 20-year old club, says playing the white tees and playing the blue tees here is like playing two different golf courses. The whites play 6,475 yards, par 72—a course well suited for big hitters. From the blues, it is 7,154 yards; this course has the length of many on the PGA Tour. Owner John Lontor takes pride in that.

There is no pro shop and no PGA pro on staff. There is a practice area, and plans call for another putting green for chipping practice. There is league play here as well as outings, and tee times are required for weekend and holiday play.

No. 1 is a par 5, though an easy one. It is 472 yards and has a small lake on the right side about 50 yards from the tee. Water shows up again a couple hundred yards out, also on the right side and reachable. Getting on this green in regulation is often dramatic. There is a big trap on the left front and the green itself is slightly elevated. It falls off steeply in the rear, and 30 yards back is a forest of tall trees.

No. 2 is a 340-yard par 4 played in the corner of the course. Woods line the right side. A creek follows the right rough, then cuts across and pools in front of the green, which is elevated. The creek continues left and circles behind. There is a big sand trap in front of this hilly green (and the greens here are not slow, by any means).

A par 3 is next, 184 yards over troubled waters. The same body of water pools in the fairway and then rolls down the left side. Players fortunate enough to hold the green have a tough putt coming up; this is another green with plenty of action.

No. 4 bends constantly left. The 402-yard par 4 starts heading for Station Road and is lined with trees on both sides.

The green is slightly elevated and has both the trademark big trap in front and the hilly green that teach caution to rash players.

No. 7 is a 518-yard par 5 that begins with a long and narrow lake right in front of the tee box. It is almost a hundred yards long, 20 yards across, and in the shape of a C. Beyond the water, a generous fairway bends a bit to the left. The back and sides of this green fall away sharply. All the greens here call for a steady hand, a sharp eye, and patience.

No. 8, a 413-yard par 4, is well defined by young trees. There is some water close to the tee on the left; it comes into play further along. At the 100-yard marker, it cuts into the fairway, then across. There is a big grass bunker to the left of the green, which is elevated slightly.

The back side opens with a 458-yard par 5. Its narrow passage to the green bends to the left and is lined with young trees. There is a small lake on the left side. More sand and a grass bunker wait at the green, a sizable putting surface that slopes forward.

No. 11, a 181-yard par 3, is a shot through a hardwood-lined hallway. On the left side is an oval pond—beyond that, deep woods. A beautiful hole. No. 12 continues around the perimeter of the course and this 390-yard par 4 continues the beauty, too. The hole bends left and, beyond the rough, the deep woods continue. The oaks here are more than a hundred feet tall.

No. 14 is a 364-yard par 4 from an especially beautiful tee box. Surrounded by those tall oaks and far from the clubhouse, this part of the course encourages players to be quiet. It is a sharp dogleg to the right, and no chance of shooting over the corner here unless one of the 14 clubs is a mortar. Both sides of the fairway lead to deep woods. Grass bunkers show up close to the green.

No. 17, the shortest par 3 here, is 161 yards to an elevated green. There is sand ten yards in front and water waits on the left and behind. The finishing hole is a 334-yard par 4, straightaway with water on the right side. Young trees line both sides of the fairway. There are several traps in the way and a shallow grass bunker on the left side of the green. It ends a long and beautiful round.

Owner John Lontor sometimes complains that his course is a well-keep secret. Behind Lontor's back, players answer that if he promoted the place at all, the secret would be out.

If it is not a well-known course, the responsibility indeed belongs to management. Naming a course Dorlon doesn't add any excitement, either. Still, it is a long and challenging 18 holes, a course for men and women who have no need for pro shops or lessons. Lontor's customers come to play.

Dorlon Park Golf Course
18000 Station Rd.
Columbia Station, OH 44028   Phone: 236-8234

Owner: John Lontor

18 holes
Tees   Yds.   Course   Slope
Middle: 6475   71   125
Back: 7154   74   131
Forward: 5691   67.4   118

Season: Apr 1–Nov 1
Hours: sunrise–sunset
Greens fees ('91): $7.00 / $14.00 wkdays; $7.50 / $15.00 wkends
Special rates: seniors: $5.00 / $10.00 until 3 p.m. wkdays
Carts: $7.00 / $14.00
Tee times: required wkends, holidays
Practice facilities: (see New Features)
Clubhouse facilities: food, beer & wine
Outings: catering available
League play: weekday afternoons
Pro shop: none
Lessons: not available
Ranger: all day
New features: chipping green, driving range

Emerald Woods Golf Course
Columbia Station

The first nine opened in 1965, and that was Audrey's. Heatherstone opened in 1967, Pine Valley opened in 1969, and St. Andrews, in 1977. General manager George Flynn is not a lifelong course manager. He was a manufacturing engineer for the better part of two decades when his layoff was announced. He told his wife it was time for a career change.

There is irrigation here but it often is used only once a week, so the dry weather can have a terrible effect on the course. "We're not as lush as some other places that water every day, but we're not burned out."

Many leagues play here and there are plenty of outings as well. "Some people at other courses tell me they're dropping outings. But I enjoy doing them, working and planning with the people who call and say 'this is my first outing.' Before I got here, I did six outings of my own."

Audrey's is listed as the No. 1 course and the opening hole, played along the entrance drive, is a 379-yard par 4. There is sand near the 150-yard marker. The hole is open until the green, which is tucked into a grove of pines.

No. 2 is a 382-yard par 4, a dogleg left that begins with a pine-lined fairway then gives way to hardwoods. In the last 130 yards to the green, the fairway is made more narrow by Lake Deborah on the right side. There is sand at this green, as well.

No. 4, a soft dogleg left, is a 400-yard par 4. It is the longest par 4 on this nine and for that reason alone the number two handicap. No. 6, a 355-yard par 4 is open, but Lake Deborah guards the left side of the green and sand sits on the right. No. 8, a 385-yard par 4, has Lake Celestine on its left.

The scorecard matches Heatherstone with Audrey's to make a round. No. 10 on Heatherstone is a 381-yard par 4, a dogleg right with plenty of room.

No. 13 is a long par 3; at 194 yards, more golfers will miss than hit the green. A hook can send the ball into an adjacent backyard, despite a wooden fence erected to prevent such shots. A sign on the fence reads: "Please, do not enter yard for your ball. Pick up good ball at pro shop counter. Thanks." On the left side of the green stands a handsome locust tree, one of many that dot the course.

No. 14 is a straight par 4, 362 yards. It is a generous hole, wide open on both sides. There is construction on the far left, part of the new nine. This green is like all the greens that preceded it: rolling and slow. George Flynn pointed out the speed is kept at the "low end of medium" and takes some adjustment. "I get some complaints, but I explain that it's just like a bowling alley. Some alleys have more oil on them, some are dryer, some are slicker. It's just a matter of adjustment."

The number one handicap on the Audrey-Heatherstone layout is No. 15, a par 4 of 445 yards. It calls for a huge drive to get in position for the approach shot. It is a soft dogleg left and trees on both sides can slow a player's progress to the egg-shaped green.

No. 16 is a par 4 of 323 yards and it gets interesting quickly. Two hundred yards out is Lake Elizabeth, which comes in from the right and crosses the fairway. A 3-wood and short iron will save the day.

No. 17 is another long par 4, 417 straight yards with just a few trees giving pause to big hitters. This green has a big, smiling sand trap with a 4-foot lip separating sand from green.

The next nine is Pine Valley, known to some players as The Nine Holes From Hell. Jungle combat experience provides the best training for this nine, which begins with the number one handicap hole, a par 4 of 353 yards. The terrain here is hilly and best covered by jeep. The woods get thick enough at times that inexperienced players need directions to the next tee. Many pack sandwiches and leave a trail of crumbs. It has some unusual holes. In short, it's a lot of fun to play.

The tee shot on No. 1 is blind. Golfers can see the first hazard, which is an opening between tall trees. The ball must pass through the trees and over a creek to an open landing area. The hole sweeps to the left and up to the green. Down the right side, the rough turns to thick underbrush; hitting through the fairway can be costly. The green has plenty of roll in it (though not fast, these greens are challenging) and a sizable sand bunker behind it. This hole calls for two very good and very accurate golf shots.

No. 2 is another blind tee shot over a creek, up a rise, and down the left side. There is a tree line along the left side—the right is wide open. Not until players find their drives is the green visible. It is hidden—really hidden—in the tree line.

No. 3 starts with a drive toward tall bushes. This hole might be played just as well by blind golfers as sighted ones. It is a par 5, a 492-yard hole that gallops without direction. The drive has plenty of landing area. The next shot, which must clear a stream and trees at water's edge, must also pay attention to Lake Kathleen on the right and keep in mind the approach. It is to a green that slopes steeply forward. Playing this hole calls for some thought. A golfer last season got to the green in regulation by hitting, in order, a 3-wood, a sand wedge, and a 7-iron.

No. 5 has the Luap Creek cutting across the fairway in front of the tee. A short par 4 of 267 yards, this dogleg left turns and rises 25 feet on its way to the green. The green is a pretty target, the rear lined with old pines. Luap Creek can continue to plague players as it winds across the fairway again in front of the green.

No. 7 is a narrow roller coaster of a hole and the green is at the bottom of several hills. A par 4 of 334 yards, the first shot is a blind one, and the next can be also. Trees make it narrow and, once in them, the only recourse is to chip back to the fairway. One more hole where players must plan the drive as carefully as the approach.

Emerald Woods Golf Course

No. 9 is an uphill par 3 of 145 yards. Club selection is vital because a wide creek cuts in front of the green.

St. Andrews is the last of the four nines (for now, anyway). It starts with a long par 4. No. 10 is a straight 421 yards with adjacent holes on both sides of the fairway. Mounds on both sides help define the hole. Closer to the green, trees make it narrow.

No. 13, a 396-yard par 4, is a blind tee shot with heavy trees and underbrush down the right side. Halfway to the hole there are mounds in the rough and water beyond the right rough. This is another fairway with unusual terrain. No. 14, a par 5 of 477 yards, is wide open for drivers and tempts players to "leave nothin' in the bag." The fairway does narrow, however, close to the green, where the creek cuts across the fairway. No. 15 is another hallway of hardwoods, a par 3 of 125 yards.

No. 16, par 5, 474 yards, has two small lakes on the right side. The one farther from the tee can be reached with a slice. The closer one accepts clubs thrown in anger or frustration. The names of the bodies of water are Lake Ball and Lake Club. The narrow fairway begins dropping the last two hundred yards. The creek cuts across just in front of the green.

No. 17, a 314-yard par 4, is a dogleg left bending around Lake Janet. The finishing hole is a 145-yard par 3, especially pretty for the water between tee and green and for the tee box itself, which has tall shade trees and a white fence on the side.

Emerald Woods has some very tough holes, though it doesn't have any long nines. It does offer a great variety. And, with a fifth nine under construction, there is more to come.

Emerald Woods Golf Course
12501 N. Boone Rd.
Columbia Station, OH 44028   Phone: 236-8940

Manager: George Flynn

36 holes	Audrey's-Heatherstone			Pine Valley-St. Andrew's		
Tees	Yds.	Course	Slope	Yds.	Course	Slope
Middle:	6165	69.1	n/r	6058	69.1	n/r
Back:	6673	71.7	n/r	6629	72.1	n/r
Forward:	5295	69.2	n/r	5080	69.4	n/r

Season: year-round
Hours: 7:00 a.m.–sunset wkdays
6:00 a.m.–sunset wkends
Greens fees ('91): Audrey's-Heatherstone: $6.75 / $13.00 wkdays; $7.25 / $14.00 wkends
Pine Valley-St. Andrew's: $7.25 / $14.00 wkdays; $7.75 / $15.00 wkends
Special rates: wkdays: 18 holes for reg. fee, $3.00 for cart (2 players), until 1:00 p.m.
seniors: $ .50 off per 9 holes, wkdays only
season pass: $625.00
Carts: $8.00 / $16.00
Tee times: taken wkends & holidays, front course only
Practice facilities: putting green
Clubhouse facilities: snack bar: food, beer, wine; 3 pavilions
Outings: special incentives for weekday outings; able to handle large groups
League play: Mon–Fri, 5:00–6:15 p.m.; one 9-hole layout always available for public play
Pro shop: lightly stocked
Lessons: not available
Ranger: evenings & wkends
Other: rental clubs available
New features: greens rebuilt: Nos. 4 & 6, back course, No. 11 front course; new executive-length 9-hole layout under construction to open late fall 1992

Erie Shores Golf Course
North Madison

Tom Weiss, PGA, has plenty to brag about at this Lake Metroparks facility. "We're certified by the state as a backyard wildlife habitat," he said. "To qualify, we planted flowers and ferns. Thirty-three species of flowers are laid out strategically to accommodate the life cycles of hummingbirds and butterflies. We have purple martin houses and bat houses and squirrel houses, as well."

This short course—5,661 yards, par 70—was developed in 1957 and the first nine holes opened in 1959. Greens fees were one dollar for nine holes. Two farms, the Atkins Farm on Lake Road East, and the Kennitz Farm, were purchased by the Erie Shores Corporation. The chicken barn from the Kennitz Farm was turned into the first clubhouse.

The park board assumed title 13 years ago. It hit the ground running and has not stopped. Construction is pending to lengthen the course to a more challenging 6,300 yards. In addition, the 1st and 9th holes will be made into a driving range, three new holes will be built or renovated, and two more practice greens will be added. The layout, he said, will be completely changed.

That will mean the plaque on the clubhouse wall with Dan Duff's course record score (61) will need an asterisk.

At present, Erie Shores (you can reach the Lake with a driver and a 6-iron) is a pretty course, well-maintained, and staffed with friendly, helpful employees. The very comfortable clubhouse seats 90, two thirds in the indoor patio and the rest in the smaller front room. The courtyard in front of the clubhouse is brick and made prettier with flowers. Every tee has a flower bed, most of them in wooden barrel halves.

When not playing, Sherri Dugan serves as gardener for the course.

Calling for tee times is an especially good idea here, as the course schedule is filled with league play, including: women, juniors, seniors, mixed couples, and, every Sunday morning, a weekend league of stalwarts. The Sunday morning league, 50 strong, is out before 7:30 a.m., and that is more than "rain or shine." It is year-round. When the greens are covered with snow, the players take shovels along with clubs.

At least once a month, Weiss puts on some sort of tournament. Night-light tourneys, the nine-hole matches played after dark, are well attended, and last year players paid to play in The Azalea Tournament. Proceeds paid for an additional 100 azalea plants.

Weiss puts a lot of time in for junior golfers. His Clubs for Kids program, in which donated clubs are cut down for junior players, provided 75 junior golfers with sets of clubs last year. In addition, for one week each year he provides free lessons for junior players.

The terrain at Erie Shores is flat, but the course offers some very pretty holes. No. 1 is a simple and short par 4, only 317 yards. A great variety of hardwoods line both sides of the first fairway, but they are not so dense as to hide an errant shot. The green has sand on the right side and the groundskeepers maintain a collar of short grass around the green. On most holes here this is about seven feet wide.

The greens here are not very fast, but they are healthy. Weiss explained that they have been allowed to grow more than is necessary because they are virtually new. A few years ago, groundskeepers used fertilizers that had been tampered with; the damage was substantial. The greens have recovered, he said, but it will be a season or two before they can be cut as close as Weiss would like.

No. 3 is a soft dogleg to the left. The tee looks out over two small lakes in front, and there is a home for purple martins. The 355-yard par 4 has a wide fairway and on some days, a ball hawker sits in the left rough and offers used balls to players. No. 4, another par 4, is almost the same length, 358 yards, and runs parallel to No. 3, so the lakes that were in front of the tee are now in front of the green.

No. 5 is a par 3 of 182 yards. Trees and heavy brush fill the right side and, closer to the green, tall hardwoods stand guard. There is sand on the right side of the green.

At No. 8 the entire tee is often completely in shadow. This par 4 of 379 yards bends softly to the left. Bird houses for chickadees and bluebirds show up here. The good-sized green has no sand traps.

No. 9, par 4, 379 yards, is typical of many holes here: very pretty tee and handsome hardwoods. The generous fairway runs straight. No. 10 is also straightaway, but a par 5 of 497 yards. There is water to the left that is easily reachable with a hook from the tee. Huge willows line the banks.

No. 13 is an easy par 4, measuring only 306 yards. The fairway bends softly to the right, and trees all the way down the right side provide direction as well as physical beauty.

The other par 5 on the back is No. 17, 451 yards. The green is tucked away on the right and to the right of the green is sand. No. 18 has water in front of the tee and along the left side. After the tee shot, players walk across a rail fence over the water to the fairway. No sand on this finishing green.

Erie Shores can be a wonderful course for family golf, where skill levels can differ greatly, but the pleasures of the course are equally enjoyed.

Erie Shores Golf Course
7298 Lake Rd. East
Madison, OH 44057   Phone: 428-3164

Manager, Pro: Tom Weiss

18 holes

Tees	Yds.	Course	Slope
Middle:	5844	66.0	108
Back:	5661	66.8	110
Forward:	4784	66.4	105

Season:	year-round
Hours:	sunrise–sunset
Greens fees:	$6.00 / $10.50 wkdays; $6.75 / $12.00 wkends
Special rates:	daily specials for seniors, women, couples all-day rates; season passes; winter rates Nov–Apr
Carts:	$4.00 / $8.00 per rider
Tee times:	taken, not required
Practice facilities:	putting green, chipping green
Clubhouse facilities:	snack bar: food, beer, wine; indoor patio
Outings:	monthly scrambles, open tournaments; private outings available
League play:	daily
Pro shop:	well stocked
Lessons:	$17.50 per 1/2 hr.; video lessons: $30.00
Ranger:	daily ranger & starter
Other:	owned by Lake Metroparks
New features:	major renovations, new holes; driving range; on-course flush restrooms, cart paths, backyard wildlife habitat

Fairway Pines Golf Course
Painesville

Fairway Pines is less than five years old, but looks and plays as if it has been around much longer. Fast greens with aprons in front, much water, judicious use of sand traps, and a very challenging layout are among its virtues. To score well, one must play very well, but it is not a course to intimidate average players. An airy, two-story clubhouse with a balcony overlooks the grass driving range and the 18th green.

Milt Johnson, PGA is the pro here. He has league play on weeknights, but Tuesday through Thursday only one side is dedicated to league play—the other nine is open. "We probably picked up more golf with the open play than with the leagues," he said. He does a good business in outings but restricts them to weekdays. The clubhouse can seat 200 when both floors are used and it is air-conditioned. A grass driving range can fit two dozen players at a time and a nearby putting green provides a good example of the greens on the course.

The course plays 5,903 yards, par 71. The front side has only one par 5 and that is quite short at 435 yards. The course can be dramatically lengthened to 6,649 by playing the blue tees. "Slow play will not be tolerated," the scorecard reads, and one of the local rules calls for playing o.b. shots stroke only, the ball to be dropped at the point of entry. Many public players play that rule anyhow, but it's nice to see it incorporated into local rules to speed play.

A grove of sycamores and willows leads to the first tee. There, next to an old-fashioned and comfortable park bench, twin garbage cans rest; players are asked to separate their trash for recycling. No. 1 is a 323-yard par 4, a slight dogleg right.

For the last hundred yards the fairway is lined on both sides with trees.

No. 2 is another par 4, this one 348 yards bending sharply to the right. A tee shot here has to be on the left side of the fairway for the best approach because in the elbow of the dogleg stands a large group of trees.

No. 3 is a handsome little par 3, 146 yards with pines and maples on both sides of the hole. The green is a sizable target with sand in the right rear. Farther back is water, but it should not come into play.

No. 4 plays 425 yards and is the sole par 5 on this side. The lake that backs up the previous green can come into play here; it is on the left side just in front of the tee. There is more water to the left of a large green.

No. 5 is the number two handicap hole. A hallway of trees leads out to this 384-yard par 4. The tee shot can intimidate players not known for accuracy off the tee, but once in the short grass it is clear sailing—except for a creek cutting across the fairway—to a large green that has no sand. The water hazard is about 165 yards from the green, though in dry weather there is no water, only a difficult lie. Closer to the green is a lake on the right side, the likely depository for an uncontrolled slice.

No. 8 is 372 yards, a par 4 that looks open from the tee but tightens with trees in last 100 yards. This is one of many tee boxes here that is especially handsome by public course standards. It is 42 yards long and only 8 yards wide. The course can play much longer and with much more challenge using the back of the box. A creek cuts across the fairway before the green, which is surrounded on three sides by tall trees.

On No. 9, a par 4 of 375 yards, it's especially important to stay out of the rough. Trees will block most shots to the green, although chipping back into play is not difficult. In front of the green is a small trap not visible until players get close.

The back side begins with a very pretty, straight par 4. For 353 yards, stands of trees on both sides add to the physical

Fairway Pines Golf Course

beauty of the course and insist on play in the fairway. The hole has a big green. Trees surround it, including a stand of white birch on the left side.

No. 11, a par 3 of 158 yards, is not difficult, but trees leaning in on the left side coupled with a creek crossing the fairway and snaking up the right side give a player plenty to worry about. There is no sand here.

The first of two par 5s on the back side is No. 12, the number three handicap hole, measuring 498 yards. Water runs down the left side behind a line of trees. There are trees on the right side as well, and a somewhat narrow fairway. Close to the green a big lake looms on the right side.

No. 13 is a par 4, 363 yards and a straight fairway to a big green. This hole is representative of the course: not difficult, very pretty, and plenty of trees on either side. There is sand on the left front of the green. No. 14 is a soft dogleg left, a par 4 of 344 yards that calls for an accurate tee shot to stay in the fairway. All of the greens here are young, of course, but they are very well maintained. The green on No. 14, no exception, is notable for its very subtle breaks.

No. 15 is only 338 yards from the white tees, but no easy par. It's a dogleg left, and blocking players who want to try cutting the corner is a stand of tall trees. An accurate tee shot is vital because the approach must clear a sizable lake waiting in front of the green. The water continues on the right side of the green.

No. 17, a par 3 of 151 yards, has a very generous green that should be hard to miss. But if they do miss, players may have to blast their way out of the sand on the right front, or chip back from between tree trunks on either side.

The last hole is another par 4 of medium length. At 344 yards, average players can do well while under the scrutiny of those resting and watching from the clubhouse balcony.

One hopes Fairway Pines is an indication of the direction public golf is going. It is a new course designed and built with the public player in mind. Neither a pushover nor a U.S.

Open layout, these 18 holes offer players plenty of opportunities for par (and bogey).

Fairway Pines Golf Course
1777 Blase-Nemeth Rd.
Painesville, OH 44077   Phone: 357-7800

Owner: Ed Tresger
Manager, Pro: Milt Johnson, PGA

18 holes

Tees	Yds.	Course	Slope
Middle:	5915	67.3	107
Back:	6649	70.9	112
Forward:	5081	68.1	106

Season: open mid-Mar
Hours: 8:00 a.m.–sunset wkdays
7:00 a.m.–sunset wkends
Greens fees ('91): $7.50 / $11.50 wkdays; $9.00 / 15.50 wkends
Special rates: seniors: $5.00 /$10.00 wkdays; $15.00 per player w/cart
Carts: $8.00 / $16.00
Tee times: taken wkends & holidays
Practice facilities: lighted natural grass driving range; putting green
Clubhouse facilities: snack bar: food, beer; banquet room
Outings: air-conditioned clubhouse accommodates 20–200
League play: Mon–Thu evenings; one 9 open to public
Pro shop: lightly stocked
Lessons: $20.00 per 1/2 hr.; daily by appointment
Ranger: daily
Special rules: non-smoking clubhouse

Forest Hills Golf Center
Elyria

The only course owned and operated by Lorain County Metroparks is this layout in Elyria. Players should take care on arrival to pull into the Forest Hills driveway and not the drive next door, which belongs to the Elyria Country Club. At Forest Hills, play can be had for about eleven dollars. At Elyria C.C., the initiation alone is twenty grand.

Frank Mittler, PGA, is the superintendent. He describes his course succinctly: "It's a good muni course with watered fairways and small, quick greens." The course also has the Black River running through it and a wealth of trees including cottonwood, walnut, buckeye, and ash. Mittler remembers when the course first opened as a nine-hole layout in 1960. "It was built by Matthew Zaleski [who also built Hilliard Lakes]. It started as a semi-private club and it had the toughest nine holes I've seen in my life."

A second nine was added after Charlie Smith bought the course in 1964. Today, the clubhouse concession is run by the father-and-son team of Gordon and Allen Freeman. Speaking of Charlie Smith, the elder Freeman said, "There's some interesting things he did with drainage tiles and irrigation and some of the stuff he pieced together. There's a section out there that he used fire hose for irrigation because he ran out of money. We don't know where he got the firehose."

They run a first-rate clubhouse and pro shop—a marked improvement, according to Mittler, over the last concessionaire. "The Freemans were instrumental in getting more leagues and more outings here. They've done so much getting the clubhouse fixed up and providing better outings."

About 25,000 rounds are played here every year. There is also plenty of league play, so calling first to ensure open play is advised. Forest Hills takes no tee times. Mittler said, "We did when we first bought it, but decided that it's a municipal golf course, so we'll go on a first-come, first-served basis. I think we pull more people in that way."

Play begins on a par 5 of 565 yards. It is a wide open hole and straight. There is an apron in front of the green and an apron, when cared for, always provides a country club look to a hole. There is sand on the left side of the green, which slopes to the rear. The greens here are very well maintained and often fast.

No. 2 shares a tee with No. 16. This 330-yard par 4 begins elevated and sweeps into a valley. The green is off to the right and is most unusual: in front is a moat-like water hazard and behind, a stand of trees. Eerily beautiful.

No. 4 shares a tee with No. 6. A 390-yard par 4, it bends to the right about halfway to the green. Hardwoods are on both sides of the fairway and nearer the green are a few huge willows. The Black River runs behind the green, then down the left side of the next hole.

No. 6 is a 365-yard par 4 that includes a dogleg left at about the 150-yard marker. The Black River shows up on this hole, too, affecting play in the last 75 yards on the right side.

No. 7 can confound and delight players. The tee shot here is crucial. It must go far enough to leave a clear approach to the small elevated green, but not so far that it tumbles into the boomerang-shaped lake that is straight out from the tee. At that point, the fairway turns left and rises. Some pines guide the hole to the green, which has no sand.

No. 9 is a 400-yard straightaway hole with a wide fairway and a green that slopes forward. Behind the green is a lake filled with bluegill and bass.

The back side begins with the number two handicap hole. No. 10 is a 445-yard par 4. Down the left side is thick underbrush and o.b. The hole bends subtly to the right on its way to a slightly rippled green.

No. 11 is a gorgeous par 3, only 135 yards The tee is elevated, the hole at the bottom of a valley. Both sides of the hole are wooded and there is a small pond to the right of the green.

No. 12 is a short par 4, only 320 yards; the hole appears wedged in the woods on the left. The right side is a bit more open and at the green are two traps.

The river glides by directly in front of the tee at No. 13, a par 4 of only 330 yards. This and the next hole play side-by-side, though they are not crowded at all; trees separate their fairways. No. 14, also par 4, measures only 285 yards. The ubiquitous Black River is on the left side of this fairway and the green here is trapped on two sides.

The final three holes play on reasonably level ground and leave the river behind. No. 16 is a 395-yard par 4 with o.b. down the left side. The fairway begins heading left before straightening out toward the green, which is mounded on three sides and backed by a stand of trees. No. 17 is straight and, again, wide open. It's only 315 yards for this par 4. No. 18 is much longer. It is a 535-yard par 5 over fairway with a few bumps, but essentially a hole marked by clear sailing.

Allen Freeman is not able to play as much as he would like, but the five-handicap player offers this observation of the course, "It's a medium-difficult course. The front nine is difficult, the back nine is easy. If you can get through the first seven holes, that's the course."

But the first seven holes include the oft-cursed No. 7, "One of the toughest in the county," according to Mittler.

Forest Hills is not a course played by Greater Clevelanders as much as it is played by Lorain County residents. They have a secret there worth protecting.

Forest Hills Golf Center
41971 Oberlin Rd. (Rte. 20)
Elyria, OH 44035   Phone: 323-2632

Managers:　　　　　Allen Freeman
　　　　　　　　　　Gordon Freeman

18 holes
Tees	Yds.	Course	Slope
Middle:	6035	68.6	115
Back:	6280	69.7	117
Forward:	4825	67.6	104

Season: Mar 14–Dec 30
Hours: 7:00 a.m.–sunset
Greens fees: $6.00 / $10.00 wkdays
$7.00 / $11.00 wkends & holidays
Special rates: wkend special: $4.00, 9 holes after 4:00 p.m.
cart special: $30.00, 2 players & cart for 18 holes (wkdays before 1:00 p.m.)
$17.00, 2 players & cart for 9 holes (wkdays before 3:00 p.m.)
seniors & juniors: $3.00 / $5.00 wkdays only
Carts: $8.50 / $17.00
Tee times: not taken
Practice facilities: putting green, practice cages
Clubhouse facilities: snack bar, half-way house: food, beer, liquor
Outings: variety of complete outing packages available
League play: various times
Pro shop: well-stocked
Lessons: not available
Ranger: daily
New features: rebuilding bunkers; automatic irrigation system

Fowler's Mill Golf Course
Chesterland

The toughest par 4 in Greater Cleveland, most players agree, is at Fowler's Mill, the course designed for TRW in 1970. When TRW operated the course, it was exclusively for company employees. When American Golf Corporation purchased it in 1986, Fowler's Mill was opened to the public.

The course was designed by Pete Dye and that signature par 4 is the 438-yard No. 4, a hole for heroes. There are just a couple of ways to succeed on that hole but a hundred ways to get in trouble. It is only one of a number of difficult holes here.

Fowler's Mill is a difficult course, not one for beginners or for those with short tempers. One of local rules here is printed on the scorecard: "The rocks and railroad ties that border lakes and rivers are considered 'margins of the hazard.' No relief."

Rob Ross manages the course and clubhouse. "My first fall here, we had some Amish fellows working here on the maintenance crew. I came in one morning not knowing they hunted the property. We opened up and I'm sending my first foursome out to the tee and I see about ten of them, with guns and hunting dogs coming down our first fairway." It is difficult enough to get over the 'opening hole jitters' without facing a passel of shotgunners.

Leagues play Fowler's Mill on weeknights. The course has two women's leagues, one that plays nine holes and the other that plays eighteen holes.

The course record is held by Lee Chill, a regular on the Ben Hogan Tour, who fired a 66 from the blue tees in the spring of 1988.

Lessons are available from pro John Paul Jones, whose counsel can be had on either the grass driving range or the sizable practice green. Even with such help, the average score here hovers around 101, Ross says. Over 35,000 rounds are played every year. Company outings are popular and the club provides everything. Two outdoor pavilions seat 200 and 150 guests, respectively.

Ross bristles at the suggestion that there might be another course prettier than his. "I think Fowler's Mill is the most scenic course in the area," he says simply.

The opening hole lends credence to his opinion. The 416-yard par 4 is a dogleg left that calls for a big drive and a big second shot. (Yardage markers are discs in the middle of the fairway. Blue is 200 yards, white is 150, red is 100.) On the right side of the dogleg is sand; on the left is a stand of trees. The hole looks more open than it plays. The green is elevated and protected with sand on the left side and trees behind it. The greens here are maintained as well as any in the area.

The infamous No. 4 fairway is narrow and dangerous. It runs along the side of large lake on the right. An inadvertent slice, however slight, can be the beginning of disaster. But bailing out to the left means no chance for par. From the tee, players must stay straight. Even a great drive is just a beginning. The approach shot, a long iron, has to be equally great. About 200 yards out, the fairway take a 90-degree right turn and continues to hug the lake. The green is protected by plenty of sand and fortified with Dye's trademark railroad ties. It would be interesting if management measured the average score on this one.

No. 5, the only par 5 here under 500 yards, is a 483-yard hole with a fairway that bends first to the left and then back to the right. It rises and falls en route to a green with plenty of sand. This hole is representative of the course in that it can't be played well by first-timers. The pleasures of playing here grows with subsequent visits, but the first round can be confounding.

No. 6 is a 407-yard par 4 that has a sharp dogleg right. For the second shot, the fairway drops at the dogleg and then rises near the green. Two traps are at the green's right side. Trees on either side of a fairway only 30 yards wide at the dogleg make this a difficult hole.

On the way to No. 7, a comparatively peaceful par 3 of 171 yards, players might reflect on the difficult last three holes. But it's a brief respite. No. 8 is a 556-yard par 5. It begins with a small valley in front of the tee and finishes with a dogleg to the left at the 150-yard marker. There is so much sand in the dogleg that an appearance by Bedouins would not surprise.

No. 9 is the first hole since No. 4 to have water, and unusual water it is. A wide creek cuts diagonally across the fairway, creating two landing areas. This 366-yard par 4 calls for a tee shot of accuracy. The approach shot also calls for judgment. The water and sand are hazards on the left.

A number of area courses are distinguished by having one side far more difficult than the other. Not so here. Both sides are hard. The front nine is called the Blue Nine, the back nine is called the White Nine. There is a third nine, the Red Nine, which is treated by most players as an oddity. It will be covered below.

The White Nine has holes numbered and handicapped one through nine. The fact that it is almost always played as the back nine is not considered on the score card.

No. 1 is a 411-yard par 4. The creek that sliced up the fairway on the last hole continues through the course and comes into play here. It will be a hazardous influence on a number of holes. Here, it cuts across the fairway and fills the left side of the green.

A walk up old wooden steps leads to No. 2, a 349-yard par 4. There is water in front, but it shouldn't come into play. The tee shot must clear a tree-lined valley. Missing to the right can send the ball into deep woods. The fairway bends slightly to the right. Two huge sand traps sit in front of the green here and a few hardwoods stand on the left.

A real premium is placed on the tee shot on No. 6, a 405-yard par 4 that is also the number one handicap on this nine. Trees guide the hole down the left side and a few tall hardwoods stand on the right. Also down the right are sand traps. The fairway is narrow and it slopes left to right. Unusual lies are not unusual here.

The last par 3 is No. 8, measuring 168 yards. While it lacks length it does not lack difficulty. In addition to a great deal of sand, the kidney-shaped green is a mere 14 yards across at its widest point.

No. 9 is a hard one to win matches on. It's a long and tough par 5 that sees few birdies. It is 544 yards long and almost impossible to reach in two. From the tee, it looks wide open, and it is, but this dogleg left has sand on the right and left sides of the fairway as well as around the green. The sand continues down the left side and the green is elevated. A par here is a great way to finish a round.

Many of the players here are ardent fans of Pete Dye's layout but know little or nothing about the third, Red, nine. That's a shame—it's gorgeous. It's across Rockhaven Road. The first tee on that side has occasional car traffic making noise behind it.

The fairway on No. 1 is well defined by greenskeeping and is wide and comfortable. This par 4, 351 yards, is a dogleg left with deep woods down the right side and a few trees on the left. In the last 100 yards the fairway narrows, turns sharply left, and rises 15 or 20 feet to the green.

No. 2 is a beautiful par 4, 393 yards and straightaway. The fairway rolls up and down and has hardwoods and deep woods on the right, a few small stands of trees on the left. The fairway drops off to the right about 100 yards from the green. From the shallow valley to the green, three sand traps are arranged staircase-style on the right.

No. 3, a magnificent par 5, is 516 yards. The fairway rises slowly and crests about 220 yards from the green. It slips gradually down to the green and narrows. Trees stand up in the left rough and create a place for Canada geese to mill about. Sand is on the left side of the green and an old hardwood grows next to it. The hole is magnificent not for the degree of difficulty but for the physical beauty of its surroundings. This nine is much quieter, most of the noise supplied by crickets.

No. 6 is a 358-yard par 4 that bends softly to the left. Old trees line both sides and a creek cuts across the fairway in front of the green. It is one of a few holes that have trees quite close to the fairway.

No. 8 is short, a 325-yard par 4 dogleg left with trees lining the hole as well as standing in the elbow. It takes a good drive down the right side to be in position for the approach shot. And the left front side of the green has not only more trees, but sand as well.

No. 9 is a 175-yard par 3. Trees line the left side of this fairway, which drops in front of the tee to rise in front of the green. It's a long and narrow green with a big dip in it halfway back on the right.

What a delightful difference between the Red Nine and the other two on the other side of the road. It shouldn't be hard to believe the same designer dreamed up all three. The aim of golf design, after all, is to create entertaining and playable courses. That was certainly done here at Fowler's Mill.

Fowler's Mill Golf Course
11595 Mayfield Rd.
Chesterland, OH 44026   Phone: 286-9545

General Manager: Rob Ross

27 holes   Blue & White   Blue & Red
Tees   Yds.   Course   Slope   Yds.   Course   Slope
Middle: 6623   72.8   133   6375   70.6   126
Back: 7002   74.7   136   6595   72.1   128
Forward: 5950   73.9   122   5913   73.6   123

             White & Red
Tees   Yds.   Course   Slope
Middle: 6226   69.5   122
Back: 6385   70.7   125
Forward: 5797   73.0   123

Season:	year-round
Hours:	sunrise–sunset
Greens fees:	$30.00 wkdays; $40.00 wkends (includes cart)
Special rates:	seniors & juniors: $8.00 for 9-hole course
Carts:	included in greens fees
Tee times:	taken, not required
Practice facilities:	range, putting green
Clubhouse facilities:	food, beer; pavilion area
Outings:	welcome
League play:	limited
Pro shop:	well stocked
Lessons:	$25.00 per 1/2 hr.; by appointment
Ranger:	daily

Gleneagles Golf Club
Twinsburg

Building and opening new public courses in northeast Ohio is exciting for the owners as well as the playing public. Creating a course during a drought adds special problems, but it hardly slowed manager Lou Catania from cutting the ribbon and sending the first foursome out onto Gleneagles in 1990.

This 18-hole layout plays 6,214 yards, par 72. The blue tees here means a round measuring 6,750 yards, a long game for all but a select few.

Ted McAnlis, of West Palm Beach, is the architect. He created a snug course that favors accuracy. Ninety is the average score of players here, though it took Walt Shirley no time at all to establish a solid course record. On August 22 of the course's first year, he fired a 66.

Catania says of the grass: "The rough is moderate, the fairways close cut and the greens soft and cut every day." On staff is Denny Appel, PGA, teaching professional. The course has a lovely driving range 400 yards deep as well as a putting green that accurately duplicates the type of green found on the softly rolling course.

The clubhouse is a one-story affair housing pro shop and eating area. Its front porch is the width of the building and a pleasant vantage point from which to watch golfers playing in on No. 9.

Perhaps new courses suffer more from weather extremes than do mature ones. The nurturing necessary for growth and development is hard to provide in the midst of a drought. Gleneagles is watered, but irrigation systems prove to be a distant second to Nature when the subject is hydration.

Gleneagles was named after the course at Gleneagles Hotel, in Perthshire, Great Britain. Its designer, James Braid, was told in the early twenties, "Make it spectacular, make it look difficult, but make it easy to get around." One wonders, after a round in Twinsburg, if Braid's ghost was leaning over designer McAnlis' shoulder.

No. 1 is a 460-yard par 5 with a sharp dogleg left. From the tee, it is a tempting view. Cutting the corner would make getting on in two a reasonable play. In the elbow is some vegetation but more of what the television golf commentators call waste bunkers. A tee shot coming up short likely won't severely punish the player. Mounds mark the right side of the fairway after the dogleg and they show up behind the green as well. The greens here are fast enough to make players pay attention and true enough that a missed putt can only be blamed on the putter. Sand sits on either side of the saddle-shaped green.

At the No. 2 tee, the scenery suddenly changes. The 353-yard par 4 has a fairway flanked by buckeye trees, maples, and shagbark hickories. It's a slight dogleg left and the hardwoods follow the bend to the green.

No. 5, a 380-yard par 4, is a slight dogleg right. From the tee, it's impossible to see any other hole. This seclusion is repeated throughout the round and provides a rich feeling of exclusivity for the player. It also further accentuates the demand for accuracy.

At the No. 6 tee, one might wish for a "Trevino fade." It's a short par 4, only 359 yards. A trap hides behind a mound at the right of the green. No. 7 is a long par 3, 190 yards that are sometimes studied by a hawk circling lazily above the fairway.

No. 8, a 473-yard par 5, leads players out of the woods and back to civilization—in this case, a housing development behind the green. But to reach the green, the ball must follow a soft bend to the right. Mounds mark either side of the fairway, and an errant shot can mean an unusual lie. The green is trapped on either side.

Gleneagles Golf Club

Going out is fun at Gleneagles, but coming in is more challenging, more beautiful, and more exciting. The No. 10 tee looks out on a fairway racing steadily downhill and sloping right. Such downhill/sidehill lies can challenge the most experienced player in any foursome. Only 371 yards, it has trouble spots enough to upset a good round. The big green is reached over a creek crossing 40 yards in front.

Just as steeply as No. 10 raced downhill, No. 11, a 323-yard par 4, staggers uphill. The final 150 yards are especially steep and lead to a green surrounded by mounds. The air space here is shared peacefully by bluebirds and bluejays.

The elevated tee at No. 12, par 4 and 393 yards, encourages thought and concentration. It looks down a steep drop to the bottom of a valley, and water, after which the fairway suddenly veers left and up. The green is large and surrounded by tall trees. This hole calls for consecutive good shots and offers little margin for error.

No. 14 is a 483-yard par 5 with deep woods along the left side and thin woods along the right. The fairway rolls downhill to a sharp dogleg left, at which point the green finally becomes visible. There's a touch of sand at the green and more troublesome mounds.

Plenty of bets will be settled on No. 18, a most unusual par 4 of 389 yards. It begins easily enough straight from the tee, but then the terrain dramatically changes. The fairway suddenly drops steeply off to the left and the remaining fairway narrows like a corset-cinched waist. The big lake on the left reaches up to the left side of the green. It bears a striking resemblance to the seaside holes at Pebble Beach.

Gleneagles is a most welcome addition to the courses here. It looks like the new kid on the block, not yet polished or confident. The course is also a lot like a custom-made suit. It looks and feels wonderful at the first fitting, but quite clearly, it will take time and professional care to bring it to perfection.

Gleneagles Golf Club
2615 Glenwood Dr.
Twinsburg, OH 44087   Phone: 425-3334

Owners: Dennis Romanini & Monte Ahuja
Manager: Lou Catania

18 holes

Tees	Yds.	Course	Slope
Middle:	6214	71.1	122
Back:	6750	73.8	130
Forward:	5210	72.6	118

Season: open mid-Apr
Hours: sunrise–sunset
Greens fees: $13.50 / $16.00
Special rates: senior rates; wkday morning specials
Carts: $16.00 for 18 holes
Tee times: required
Practice facilities: range, putting & chipping green
Clubhouse facilities: covered porch; party tent for up to 200 people
Outings: corporate or group outings; cookouts, buffets
League play: Mon–Fri 4:00–6:30 p.m.
Pro shop: well stocked
Lessons: by appointment
Ranger: daily
New features: enlarged tees; new sand bunkers

Grantwood Recreation Park
Solon

This course is a barn-burner. Literally. A dozen years ago, the city of Solon purchased from private owners 18 holes on Aurora Road and created Grantwood Recreation Park. The course, originally built as a nine-hole layout in the twenties, used an old barn for its clubhouse.

In 1981, a new clubhouse and banquet facility went up; a party was held to celebrate the opening. Among the honored guests were the Solon Fire Department. And a highlight of the party was the burning down of the old clubhouse.

While it is owned by the city, Grantwood is not subsidized by taxpayers. Operating funds come only from greens fees, services of the banquet facilities, and pro shop receipts.

Since the town bought it, the course has undergone substantial change. The change continues. Last year new red tees were installed. "The tees weren't fair for lady players," Dennis Smith, PGA, said. Smith is the assistant pro at the club. Other work included planting 200 trees, expanding some greens, and installing more sand traps. It is a busy course, Smith noted, and most of the work was done not to make play more difficult, but to make it safer. Designs for cart paths are on the drawing board.

Tee times are strongly recommended here. More than 35,000 rounds are played every year and leagues constitute a good part of that: industrial, seniors, women's, and traveling leagues all enjoy Grantwood.

The clubhouse does a good banquet business, and golf outings and fund raisers are often held here. The facilities, the location, and the excellent parking make it useful year-round as well.

For all the rounds played here, Smith estimates the average scores to be between 95 and 105. That average could be lowered, perhaps, if players were to take advantage of the teaching programs offered at Grantwood. Lessons are available for individuals and groups. Video tape and swing analysis are available. Head pro Bob Garrett, PGA, shares the course record of 63 with a few others. Maybe that's one good reason to have him analyze your swing—Smith only fired a 65.

The rough is allowed to grow between 2 1/2" and 3" and water comes into play on eleven holes. The course is bisected by a railroad line, which players cross under via an old tunnel. Rich Gray tells of once landing a drive in a slow-moving coal car headed east—his longest drive ever. It must be pointed out, though, that eventually that drive went out of bounds. And out of state. The railroad line is no longer in use and the tunnel under it adds a bit of charm to the layout.

No. 1 is wide open with a trap about 140 yards out. It plays 390 yards, a good warm-up hole. It's difficult to lose a ball on this hole, though the second shot is blind because of the rolling fairway. Better here to ignore the checkered aiming flag and instead shoot for the birdhouse, designed for those great mosquito-eaters: purple martins. Traps protect both sides of the green.

No. 2 is the number two handicap and plays 408 yards. Water cuts across the fairway a hundred yards in front of the green. No. 3, a short par 4 of 262 yards, is a dogleg right with trees protecting the entire right side. There is some water about 120 yards from the green and two sand traps at the green.

The first par 3 is No. 4. When pin placement is behind one of two traps, the 150-yard hole (all uphill) presents a challenge.

After five holes, it's through the tunnel, where traffic to many holes converges. The holes run parallel on this side, but it's not crowded. There is enough rough and space between fairways to minimize shooting into (and from) adjacent fairways. This side of the course is carved out of rich farmland and the thick growth around its edges gives it a stadium-like feel. With the old-growth hardwoods, it's more impressive than the other, more open side of the tracks.

The two par 5s on the front side are consecutive. No. 6 is almost a hundred yards longer than No. 7, which plays 465 yards. It is No. 7 that is the more interesting, however, because it tempts big hitters to send the second shot to the green, and that shot is blind. The fairway rises gently, dips and bends softly left, and narrows all the way to the green. A bell at this green would make putters feel a bit more secure and, for players approaching, eliminate the need to run up and check for a cleared green. And bells add such a graceful touch to courses.

No. 8 is the third par 3 on the front side and was closed much of 1991 for major reconstructive surgery. During that period, the starter reminded players to play two balls at No. 17, the last par 3, and one whose distance from the white tees is similar to No. 8. Good thinking on the part of management.

No. 10 looks more difficult than it plays, though it has the edge of a lake on the left side. This 343-yard par 4 is a dogleg right. No. 11 is another short par 4 but of careful design. A big drive on this 287-yard dogleg left can go through the fairway. The green is elevated.

The number one handicap, No. 13, calls for a big hit from the tee. Carry must be more than 200 yards to clear the water on this 410-yard par 4 that bends to the right 170 yards from the green.

No. 17, a par 3, tempts adventurous players to hit from the blues even if they are playing the whites. The blue tee is 250 yards—all over water—from the green. The white tees are 100 yards shorter but still over part of the lake.

The pro shop is stocked with every major brand of club, extensive men's and women's golf wear, and almost 400 pairs of spiked shoes. For those of us who are regularly tempted to toss our putters into the lake, almost 300 putters are offered. None comes guaranteed, but each comes with hope.

Grantwood Recreation Park
38855 Aurora Rd.
Solon, OH 44139   Phone: 248-4646

Manager, Pro: Bob Garrett, PGA

Tees	Yds.	Course	Slope
Middle:	6063	69.9	121
Back:	6374	71.4	123
Forward:	5607	72.5	124

Season:	Apr–Nov
Hours:	sunrise–sunset
Greens fees:	$8.00 / $13.50 wkdays
	$9.00 / $17.00 wkends & holidays
Special rates:	seniors: $32.50 for 2 players w/cart, wkdays
Carts:	$16.00
Tee times:	taken
Practice facilities:	putting green, chipping green, practice sand
Clubhouse facilities:	food, beer
Outings:	catered in either banquet hall or shelter house
League play:	wkdays
Pro shop:	well stocked
Lessons:	by appointment
Ranger:	all times
New features:	finishing touches being added on $1 million improvement project that includes new cart paths, additional sand traps and grass bunkers, over 300 new trees, automatic sprinkling system, enlarged greens, new women's tees, new gold (senior) tees

Highland Park Golf Course
Highland Hills

The cover photo on the scorecard here is a hint. In the foreground, next to a sand trap, a whole generation of bright yellow dandelions blooms.

The course and the facilities, owned and operated by the City of Cleveland, are not well cared for. Joe Mossbrook, veteran television reporter, said while playing last summer: "It was one of the better municipal courses in the country in the sixties. What happened was [former mayors] Stokes and Perk started taking money out of the golf courses to balance the budget and this one went to pot, they just let it go down hill."

Ed Rahel, current commissioner of urban forestry for the city, said the same thing in another language. "Through the years, the Recreation Department, supported by tax dollars through the General Fund, enhanced their programming by using funds generated by the golf courses, instead of putting the monies back into the respective course. The deteriorated condition of the course, especially Highland, shows the toll this practice has taken."

The commissioner said the two Cleveland courses, Highland Park and Seneca, are now "enterprise accounts," which means they operate as independent business entities. This is hopeful. Each "runs as its own business, living off its own proceeds and paying its own way. Everything from personnel, materials and supplies, equipment, and even capital improvements to the courses are to be financed by fees generated at the courses."

Highland, where it appears no capital improvements have been made since the sand wedge was invented, is undergoing important change. In 1992, the fairway irrigation project is to be finished and in 1993, a new clubhouse is planned. The old clubhouse is a firetrap and the men's locker room is generally filthy. The improvements will help, but if Highland is to climb back to respectability, it will have to attract more than 14,000 18-hole rounds a year. Other, nearby courses, with higher greens fees, do more than twice that business.

Highland was built in 1912 and opened for play in 1913. It's really a fine layout; in the mid-sixties, the Cleveland Open was played here and won by "Champagne" Tony Lema. There is a Blue Course and a Red Course. The Red is almost 400 yards shorter than the Blue, but neither is short.

The Blue course does not turn at the clubhouse and so does not lend itself to nine-hole play. It opens with a 393-yard par 4 from an elevated tee that looks down on a fairway lined with trees. The terrain continues down until, at about the 150-yard mark, a creek cuts across. On the other side, the ground rises suddenly to a green with sand around the right side and rear.

No. 2 is a 408-yard par 4 and, like many of the holes here, straight. On the right side of the fairway is a cemetery, and at the green there is sand right and left. No. 3 is the number one handicap, a par 4 of 454 yards. The fairway rolls a bit on this and many holes at Highland, but the only drama here is provided by length. The fairway is generous and straight to the green, which has a grass bunker in front and seven white oaks like sentinels behind.

The only par 5 on the front side is No. 7, an attractive 553-yard hole that begins at an elevated tee, drops 30 feet into a valley and stays there until it reaches the green, which rises to the level of the tee. There is water here, including a stream that cuts across the fairway about 200 yards before the green.

No. 8 runs parallel to the old Warrensville Workhouse, a light security prison no longer in operation. A 367-yard par 4, it bends left at the 150-yard marker. The corner can be cleared with a big drive, but hooking the ball will send it into the ex-prison's backyard. Near the 150-yard marker is a large fairway bunker and, at the green, more sand on the left side.

The front side ends with a long, 431-yard par 4. It is straight and runs along the edge of the course. The left side has hardwoods but the right side is open. Near the green is an unusually shaped sand trap. It appears to be a silhouette of Bullwinkle, cartoon partner of Rocket J. Squirrel. There is a small snack bar here and two portable toilets.

The back side wends its way to the clubhouse. No. 10 is a gorgeous par 4, a straightaway 400 yards with trees lining the fairway once the hole gets under way and plenty of sand at the green. A simple hole, to be sure, but brightened with all the green that Nature provides, the symmetry of the hole is easy to appreciate.

No. 12 is a short par 4, only 337 yards, but blessed with hilly terrain and a green with dramatic fall-off on the left side. There is a lot of sand at the green and an American elm stands at the left rear.

No. 16 is a 479-yard par 5 with a water fountain at the tee box. Though technically not part of the irrigation project, its pressure is such that the back of the tee box can be watered from ten or twelve yards away. This is a straight hole with sand on the right side of the green.

No. 17 has the graveyard on the left side and is a long 444 yards from tee to well-bunkered green. This par 4 is the number two handicap hole.

The 18th hole on the Blue course is only the number four handicap hole, but it is a hole on which matches are decided. A long and dangerous par 4 of 449 yards, it begins with a tee shot into a valley that has a creek running diagonally across the fairway. On the other side of the creek the fairway leans to the left and rises to an elevated green. It's a finishing hole of U.S. Open proportions.

The Red Course is decidedly different. The hilly terrain comes into play more than it does on the Blue. Both nines finish at the clubhouse. And the Red Course finishes with a pair of par 4s totaling only 729 yards.

No. 1 is a blind tee shot. A par 4, it is 388 yards over an up-and-down fairway. It rises from the tee and crests at about 200 yards and then falls steadily until 50 yards from the green, where it rises again. This hole could use a bell to ring to let players on the tee know when it is safe to hit. A ranger could fill the same need, but neither is provided.

The 4th tee is reached after a short walk through the woods. This par 5 is 480 yards and straight as the crow flies. For golfers, however, the wide fairway drops suddenly at the 150-yard marker. All the way down the right side is deep woods; a line of trees marks the left side. Forty yards from the green, a long and narrow trap runs down the right rough and continues past the green.

No. 6 looks easy on the scorecard: a par 4 of only 264 yards. But the fairway near the green slopes right to left, presenting difficult uphill/sidehill lies for the approach shot. Mature hardwoods surround the green and knock errant shots out of the air. There is also sand at the rear of this green.

No. 8 begins with a tee box obviously used for tank maneuvers. It is yet another blind tee shot with thick woods down the left side and open area on the right. A 402-yard par 4, it's the number one handicap hole on the Red Course. It is number one because it has a blind tee shot, a hilly fairway, and a green that cannot be safely reached except by air. About 40 yards in front of the green, the left side of the fairway suddenly drops, cliff-like, about a dozen feet. Bouncing this ball onto the green is out of the question. And the green, sitting in a shallow valley, is the toughest at Highland. The right side is two or three feet higher than the left. At the left rear, the ground suddenly rises and on the right is a stand of trees. A tough pin placement can easily add three or four strokes to a score. A par on No. 8 is something to talk about.

No. 9 is a 167-yard par 3 that has a big, generous green with some sand at the right rear. The tee provides a nice view of both the hole and the dilapidated clubhouse behind the green.

No. 10 is a 391-yard par 4 lined with trees on both sides. It plays downhill to a creek cutting across and then, 40 or 50 yards from the elevated green, the fairway jumps up. The green has sand on both sides. With rollicking fairway, water hazard, elevated green with sand, and almost 400 yards of hole, a great deal of golf is packed in to this par 4.

No. 14, the lone par 5 on this side, is 498 yards long and quite straight. It is a blind tee shot, however, as the first hundred yards feature a creek cutting across the fairway and then terrain jumping up 10 or 15 feet. It is a wide and generous fairway. A stand of hardwoods is behind the flat green.

No. 15 is yet another hole with a fairway to make a topographer dizzy. It's a 356-yard par 4 and from the tee the fairway immediately dips and narrows. Hip-high rough on the right and a few heavy hardwoods on the left underline the importance of playing from the fairway. In the deep rough on the right side, a creek appears and cuts across the fairway about 40 yards from the green. At the green there is sand in front with a steep lip to clear. On the Red Course, it's the number two handicap hole.

No. 16 is the only par 3 on this side, but at 237 yards, it's all the par 3 this side needs. No. 18 is a straight but bumpy ride of 403 yards along a wide fairway that dips, then rises, in front of the green. Caution: fly the green and you might bring down the clubhouse.

All in all, Highland could be among the area's best. It just needs a commitment to golf on the part of the owners.

Highland Park Golf Course
3550 Green Rd.
Highland Hills, OH 44122   Phone: 561-6270

Manager: Andre Springs

36 holes	Red Course			Blue Course		
Tees	Yds.	Course	Slope	Yds.	Course	Slope
Middle:	6341	69.7	113	6709	71.7	119
Forward:	5945	73.1	119	6289	75.7	125

Season: spring–fall
Hours: 6:00 a.m.–8:00 p.m.
Greens fees: $7.00 / $12.00
Special rates: senior rates
Carts: $4.50 / $8.00
Tee times: taken for blue course
Practice facilities: putting green, chipping green
Clubhouse facilities: food, beer, liquor
Outings: regular course events only; call for details
League play: various times
Pro shop: lightly stocked
Lessons: $20.00 per 1/2 hr.; by appointment
Ranger: various times
New features: continued work on irrigation system; new construction planned for clubhouse

Hilliard Lakes Golf Course
Westlake

The first nine holes were built here in 1968, the second finished in 1974. It's a tight and flat course with plenty of water. Accuracy is more valuable than length and a good short game pays substantial dividends.

And owner Ron Zaleski is in the middle of a program to make accuracy yet more valuable. He has filled about five dozen new bunkers with sand and placed earthen mounds at strategic points throughout the course. He is in the process of making the course longer, too. "To be realistic, it'll be a few years before we get it completed."

Tee times are not taken and outings are not held. There are both practice green and practice fairway. The clubhouse and pro shop are in a handsome brick building and the enclosed porch has room for a few dozen players.

Zaleski tells of a regular player, a man who showed up daily on the tee. "I mean, I saw this guy every day. I saw him more than I saw my wife. And then for two weeks I didn't see him." At the end of two weeks, he showed up again. " 'John,' I said, 'where you been?' He said, 'Well, my wife said it's either golf or her.' "

It took him two weeks to move out and start legal proceedings. "And that's a true story," Zaleski said.

No. 1 is a par 5 of 476 yards starting at a well-manicured tee box reached by stairs made of railroad ties. A stand of oaks provides shade. There is water on the far left of the hole and a canal moseys across about 100 yards from the green then flows up and to the right side of the green. The generous fairway bends just a bit to the right. There is sand before and at the green, a big one with plenty of roll in it.

A bridge leads players to the next tee. The canal runs almost parallel to No. 2, making a water shot for slicers a certainty. But this 360-yard par 4 is not going to be tough for accurate shooters. The fairway bends to the left and some tall trees come into play on both sides. Mounds line the rough and there is plenty of sand at the large green.

On No. 4, a par 4 of 354 yards, the drive must again clear the canal. It's a narrow, tree-lined fairway, but there is no underbrush or thick shrubbery to hide the ball. A note: some holes here don't have 150-yard markers, but 135-yard markers. The markers are not always easy to find because they are white discs nailed to trees. But the measurements are suspect.

No. 5 is a 160-yard par 3. The large green is well-bunkered and elevated, and the surrounding trees, especially several old willows on the right, help make it a beautiful hole.

No. 8 is another hole with new fairway sand and mounds. There is water on the left of this par 4 of 385 yards. No. 9, a long par 3 of 190 yards, is mostly over water and ends near the clubhouse porch.

The back side begins with a straight par 4 of 410 yards. Thick woods on the left and tall trees on the right make it narrow for the first hundred yards. On the left is o.b. The hole opens up quite a bit after the drive, though. The rough is marked with mounds.

No. 11, a 497-yard par 5, continues in the same direction, so the left side continues to be o.b.—a recently constructed housing development is there. A half-dozen fairway traps rest between the 150-yard marker and the green.

No. 14, a 365-yard par 4, is a good driving hole and accepts fades graciously. Anything more than that, however, leads to a chip back into the fairway. While the left has room, the hole bends to the right toward a steeply sloped putting green.

No. 16 tee is reached by walking around a frog pond. The tee is new and the drive now has to clear water to get to a small landing area. Once that shot is made, it's a straight line to the green. The canal shows up again on the right side, water and o.b. on the left, and there is sand at the green.

Hilliard Lakes Golf Course

No. 18 has a very generous fairway. The hole is long at 410 yards, and the par 4 has mounds and trees on both sides. The green is protected by four sand traps.

Hilliard Lakes is a course of many virtues, an easily walked layout with plenty of sand and water, mounds and trees. And management continues to improve it—not by expanding, but by developing what is already there. Construction efforts—lengthened holes, new hazards—look to a bright future.

Hilliard Lakes Golf Course
31666 Hilliard Blvd.
Westlake, OH 44145   Phone: 871-9578

Manager: Ron Zaleski

18 holes
Tees	Yds.	Course	Slope
Back:	6600	69.5	122
Forward:	6200	71.5	120

Season:	Mar–Dec
Hours:	sunrise–sunset
Greens fees:	n/a
Special rates:	none
Carts:	n/a
Tee times:	not taken
Practice facilities:	range, putting green
Clubhouse facilities:	snack bar
Outings:	available
League play:	contact course for times
Pro shop:	well stocked
Lessons:	by appointment; $25.00 per 1/2 hr.
Ranger:	daily
New features:	adding over 200 pine trees; lengthening par 5s, completed fairway watering system last year

Hinckley Hills Golf Course
Hinckley

This challenging and hilly course is a tough one to walk. Designed by the late Harold Paddock, Sr., and opened in 1963, It plays 6,248 yards, most of them uphill, downhill, or sidehill.

Those numbers are from the white tees. From the blue tees, it plays 6,704 yards, par 73 (there is a second par 5 on the back). There are no women's tees at Hinckley, according to manager Sue Smith, the stern mistress of golf, who lectures, "They're not women's tees, they're forward markers and they're very adamant about those now. Because seniors and juniors use them, you'd better get that story straight."

The pro shop/clubhouse has been expanded and improved in recent years and combines with a nearby pavilion to provide services, including outings, that are first rate. The course is filled with hills, water, big greens, sand, and on two holes, natural gas wells. Free drops from the wells.

The course wastes no time in showing off its virtues. No. 1 is a 510-yard par 5 from an elevated tee. The wide fairway sweeps up and down, then up and down again as it makes its way to an elevated green. Trees fill both sides of the last hundred yards.

No. 2 is more of the same, a 476-yard par 5 parallels the first fairway. Although this hole is shorter than the previous one, getting on in two is extremely difficult because the fairway rises the last 200 yards. At the green are sand traps on both sides.

No. 3, a 432-yard par 4, starts with a blind tee shot. Many of the tee boxes here provide striking views of the surrounding countryside and this is one of them. After the first 100 yards, the fairway is marked by two large mounds on either side, then runs downhill until the last 150 yards, where it flattens out to a green with no sand.

These first three holes provide a good introduction to the course. While neither short nor easy, Hinckley does play wide open. Length here is slightly more valuable than accuracy.

No. 4 is a 331-yard par 4 marked with trees down the right side. The fairway drifts down to a large green that has an equally large sand trap guarding the right front quarter. The hole appears to be a respite, especially after the first three holes, but the large green is a bit deceiving: it falls off severely in back and is filled with subtle and not-so-subtle undulations.

No. 5 is another par 4, parallel to the previous hole. As the last hole went downhill, this one rises. A straightaway 354 yards, it plays much longer than the scorecard might indicate. Up to the 150-yard marker, deep woods line the left side, though it is still a generous fairway. A line of trees follows down the right side and the green is marked on both sides with large mounds.

The up-and-down nature of the course continues at the tee on No. 6, a beautiful 143-yard par 3. It is downhill to a large green backed by hardwoods and then a valley. Signs are nailed into the trees reminding riders that the terrain is "Not safe for golf carts."

No. 8 is a par 3 that calls for a good shot with the proper club. Only 147 yards, it is steeply uphill and players who did not take notice of the flag position when they were on the nearby No. 2 tee will see the flag but not know how deeply the pin is placed. A grass bunker slows a few balls hit to the right front of the green. Big, high slices can land on the No. 2 tee, further upsetting players who have enough to worry about, having just finished No. 1.

Twenty-four yards of turf, the difference between the white tees and the blue tees, is substantial yardage if the hole is a par 3 or par 4, but on this next, legendary par 5, it's not much.

Hitting from the white tees on No. 9 begins a journey of 598 yards. Hitting from the blues is 622 yards. Regardless of starting point, the hole is tough. Not just because of the length, but because the fairway, which rises and falls steeply, provides players with difficult uphill and downhill lies. It is a straight hole, o.b. all the way down the left side. To make it more scenic, a three-acre lake bed was just excavated and allowed to fill with spring water and runoff. It is on the left side of the fairway at the bottom of the elevated tee.

Players new to the course might be surprised, on glancing at the scorecard, that No. 9 is only the number two handicap hole. The number one handicap waits on the back side.

No. 11, a par 5, provides another striking view from the tee. The hole is downhill for 476 yards. This is one of the few holes here where accuracy off the tee is more important than anything else. As the fairway drops, stands of trees show up on both sides. About a hundred yards from the green is a sand trap on the right side. On the left, as trees close in for the final 150 yards, a ravine appears. To the left of the green is sand.

Management believes the toughest hole on the course is No. 12, a 448-yard uphill dogleg par 4. It may be the number one handicap hole in all of Medina County. From the tee it's a blind shot up a steeply rising fairway. Tall hardwoods the first hundred yards on both sides make it feel like teeing off with Mother Nature. The dogleg, about halfway to the hole, goes right. There is a J-shaped trap on the right side, hidden from the tee, but easily found by those who slice off the tee.

That which goes up, even at Hinckley Hills, must come down. No. 13 is a 309-yard par 4 tumbling from an elevated tee to a star-shaped green. Between each point on the star is a sand trap.

The first par 3 on this side is No. 15, a short 120 yards to a green with a gaping sand trap on the right front. Big trees back up this green and bound the left side as well.

No. 16 is a 389-yard par 4 when played from the white tees, but a 495-yard par 5 when played from the blues. Heavy

Hinckley Hills Golf Course

woods and deep trouble line the right side of this hole, and the left side is comparatively clear. The terrain rises from the blind tee shot and rolls up and down on its way to the green, which features large sand traps on both sides.

No. 17, a 140-yard par 3, is gorgeous. Players fire across a lake to a fairway that suddenly rises to an elevated green. A huge sand trap dominates the left front and a second trap marks the right side. It's not unusual to see trout drifting along in the lake. The left side of the landing area is filled with trees, which protect the nearby 18th tee.

The finishing hole is a 345-yard par 4 that begins with a little water in front of the tee and then rises and heads for home. A few trees are on the right and a small lake, as well. In the narrow lake is a tiny green island (not a part of the hole). Temptation to shoot for it is too much for many players, even though their balls are then lost.

Hinckley Hills is one of five public courses in tiny Hinckley, Ohio. Its big layout calls for length, accuracy, and a very good short game. It impresses regulars as well as first-time players. Well it should. It is, quite simply, a lot of golf course.

Hinckley Hills Golf Course
300 State Rd.
Hinckley, OH 44233   Phone: 278-4861

Manager: Sue Smith

18 holes

Tees	Yds.	Course	Slope
Middle:	6248	69.0	113
Back:	6704	71.4	121
Forward:	5478	70.2	114

Season: Apr 1–Nov 15
Hours: sunrise–sunset
Greens fees ('91): $9.00 / $18.00
Special rates: 2 players w/cart: $24.00 / $48.00 (wkdays and after 2 p.m. on wkends and holidays)
Carts: $9.00 / $18.00
Tee times: taken wkends
Practice facilities: driving net; 2 putting greens
Clubhouse facilities: snack bar: food, beer, liquor; party room; pavilion
Outings: available
League play: daily
Pro shop: lightly stocked
Lessons: not available
Ranger: certain days only
New features: new lake on No. 9

Ironwood Golf Course
Hinckley

It's not the greens. Not the sand. Not the narrow fairways. And it's not the hills. The worrisome element at Ironwood is the lightning.

Owner Bob Brown explained, "We've been hit a number of times. We're sitting on top of the hill, so high that it's blown the transformer off. It's blown out the telephones. I mean it literally blew the wires apart. It's blown out the wall pump in our water well, and the heating element in the hot dog cooker. We're just high on the ridge here. In fact, over there across the valley is the highest point in the county and we're definitely not much under it."

But while the odds of being struck by lightning are better than the odds of winning the Ohio lottery, that's no reason to shy away from this first-rate track.

Ironwood was laid out by the late Harold Paddock, a designer who also helped create Hinckley Hills and other courses. He was in a wheelchair by the time he worked on Ironwood. The first nine holes opened in 1967; the back nine opened a year later.

Over 20,000 rounds are played here each year. There is plenty of league play, including traveling leagues on the weekends. Tee times are taken for weekend play but are unnecessary weekdays. The pro shop is in one end of a clubhouse that seats more than 80. It's a very well-stocked shop, but because quality costs, it's expensive. Top of the line clubs and equipment are featured.

Women are welcomed at Ironwood (there are two women's leagues playing here), but as Brown says, "It's a pretty tough course for the ladies. They don't get the big yardage they probably should have."

It's a pretty tough course for men, too. From the white tees, it plays 6,042, par 71. Three of the par 4s on the front side are longer than 420 yards. No. 1 is one of them. It is 431 yards, all downhill, to a green that falls away on the sides. The entire right side of the hole is o.b. and trees mark the left side. The view of the valley from the first tee is magnificent. The first green is sizable.

Behind the first green is the tee for No. 2, a par 3 of more than 200 yards, again downhill. On both sides of the steep fairway are woods. So the tee calls for more than a big hit—it also has to be accurate. This green is also substantial. But it is sloped steeply and getting a tee shot to stick here is no guarantee of par. The sides of the green, especially in the back, fall away.

No. 4 is a 340-yard par 4, a generous fairway. But the fairway, which rises quickly, leans to the right and makes slices act like unruly children. At the tee is a small pond and a sign stuck in the bank: "Lake Aquilino," it reads. Most approach shots are made with the ball lower than the feet of the player and can lead to trouble. The green is steeply slanted and difficult.

No. 7, a 455-yard par 5, is the climb out of the valley. The fairway is wide open at the tee but narrows considerably as it gets closer to the green. Stands of old and tall hardwoods mark the fairway at 200 and 150 yards. The fairway, which has been rising steadily, suddenly rises much faster. The green is back on the top level, not far from the clubhouse.

To play the second nine, it's back into the valley. No. 10 is a 368-yard par 4, all downhill. No. 11, still downhill, is a par 3 of 171 yards. The penalties for a poor tee shot are severe: the green is protected by a pond in front; on both sides are hardwoods and thick brush. This green slopes slightly forward.

No. 14 is the first of two unusual holes. The tee shot on this 359-yard par 4 must avoid water in front of the tee and more water on the right side in the landing area. The left side is more open than the right, where there are dense woods, but is still not wide. The approach shot has to reach a much elevated green. To make the shot more interesting, at the bottom of the green on the left side is a sizable pond. The fairway narrows to 30 yards. At the green, woods line the rear and right side. There's no sand here, but that is small comfort. Players might not usually brag about getting on a 359-yard par 4 in regulation, but this may be an exception.

No. 15, a 316-yard par 4, is even more narrow. From the elevated tee to the canal crossing the fairway is 210 yards. Laying up to that point can be wise; there are a only few more yards of landing area on the other side of the water before a steep rise toward the green. This is not the hole for trying out a new driver. The approach has woods on both sides.

No. 17 is an uphill par 3 of 138 yards. The walk up continues behind the green to the No. 18 tee. This final hole is a 454-yard par 5 and an uphill dogleg left. In the elbow is a stand of oaks and a pond. Playing uphill on the last hole may call for an extra club or two.

Ironwood opens April 1 and closes the second week of November. Outings are no longer held here ("They're a hassle"), though Bob Brown welcomes small golf parties.

He has enough to worry about. Maintaining the course, with its hills and valleys and ponds, is job enough. The ponds supply water for the course, so it suffers much less than others with only municipal water during drought periods.

Ironwood Golf Course
445 State Rd.
Hinckley, OH 44233   Phone: 278-7171

Owner / Manager: Bob Brown

18 holes

Tees	Yds.	Course	Slope
Middle:	6042	68.3	115
Back:	6360	69.7	118
Forward:	5785	72.8	124

Season: Apr 4–Nov 8
Hours: sunrise–sunset
Greens fees: $15.00 wkdays; $17.00 wkends
Special rates: seniors: $20.00 per person, 18 holes & cart
Carts: $18.00
Tee times: required wkends until 1:00 p.m.
Practice facilities: putting & chipping green
Clubhouse facilities: snack bar
Outings: golf only; no picnic outings
League play: every evening
Pro shop: well stocked
Lessons: not available
Ranger: daily

Lost Nation Municipal Golf Course
Willoughby

Lost Nation, built in 1928, has weathered wars, recessions, the Depression, good times and bad, and . . . weather. Every once in a while, someone bounces a ball on the ice in front of No. 7 and aces the par 3.

At least that's what Gordon Haworth said. The manager runs a busy course from his office, part of an old hunting lodge. Lessons are available here, both individual and group. And a junior program is well under way. Tee times are taken on weekends and holidays and outings are popular here.

It's a reasonably flat course, and except for Nos. 1 and 9, the front nine is played on the other side of Hodgson Road. No. 1 is a 385-yard par 4. It begins just outside the clubhouse and heads for the Lost Nation Airport in the distance. It bends to the right toward a small green with a couple of traps on the right side. The hole is fairly open, with a driving range on the left and the entrance drive on the right.

The tee box for No. 2, the shorter of the par 5s on the front side, is found across the road and next to the airport. Like the previous hole, it bends to the right and is endowed with plenty of fairway and manageable rough. Down the left side is o.b., and the signs on the airport property promise to prosecute trespassers. On both sides of the fairway are mounds; at the green, big sand traps sit on both sides.

No. 3, a 140-yard par 3, continues along airport property. It is an easy par 3, hardwoods on the right side and behind the green. There is no sand here.

At No. 4, the golf gets more challenging. It's a 400-yard par 4, a slight dogleg left. The left side is filled with thick woods and, before the 150-yard markers, big grass bunkers sit on both sides of the fairway. A few more bunkers appear at the green—one grass and one sand.

No. 5, a 475-yard par 5, has a sneaky little water hazard that begins as a creek cutting across the fairway in front of the women's tees. When it finds the left rough, it turns up toward the green. On the right side of the fairway, big grass bunkers slow balls headed for the adjacent sixth fairway. Players with well-developed slices will share fairways on these two holes.

No. 7 is the par 3 that can be aced in winter via the ice. A great deal of winter golf is played here. That sounds unlikely, given the easterly location and nearness to the snow belt, but the winds coming in off the lake push the snow farther south. This is a 155-yard shot that often sails over the heads of Canada geese who have taken up residence at the water. Haworth said the greens here are built on soil, not sand, and he figures they would rate a 7 on the Stimpmeter.

No. 8 is a 375-yard par 4 that starts open, then is edged by hardwoods and thick brush on the right side. On the left is housing, o.b. Twenty and 30 yards from the green, sand bunkers wait in ambush. The trap on the right can be particularly troublesome as it can call for lofting a ball 8 feet just to clear the bunker.

Then it's back across Hodgson Road to the tee at No. 9, a 320-yard par 4 that bends off to the right. There are thick woods on the left and a long line of telephone poles marking the right. The terrain becomes uneven near the green and nearby traps are indeed hazardous. It's not a long hole by any means, but playing it casually can suddenly add several strokes to the score.

The back nine opens and closes with par 5s. It is the more difficult nine, because woods and water play a more important role and the terrain rises and falls more on this side of the road.

No. 10 is a 455-yard par 5. It plays along the edge of the course (as do the next three holes). For players who can keep the ball in the short grass, it's not a tough hole. But deep woods line the left side and circle behind the green. The fairway rises 10 or 12 feet a hundred yards out. After that it is open and straight.

No. 13, a 350-yard par 4, has a wide creek just in front of the tee. The hole bends right and a hook here will wind up off the course. The fairway rises dramatically 50 yards out from the tee and the left side is filled with sand and grass bunkers. The rough here is especially rough.

No. 14 is only 325 yards and plays in a valley that falls from an elevated tee and rises a hundred yards later to a level fairway and the green. The valley should not cause problems, though the S-shaped creek in it gives players on the tee pause. The hole is something of a relief between the previous hole and the next one, actually. No. 15, a 415-yard par 4, is the number one handicap. Woods on both sides make the fairway narrow, and a big creek 130 yards in front of the elevated green only adds to the challenge.

No. 18 is a 475-yard par 5 with grass fairway bunkers. There is water in front of the small green, behind which sand will slow balls headed for the clubhouse.

Lost Nation is a course with some very tough holes and plans to expand. Another nine has been drawn. How the course got its name is a matter of conjecture. Haworth said the name comes from an Indian tribe that found itself lost in these parts. That's hard to believe, given the nearness of both State Route 2 and Interstate 90.

Lost Nation Municipal Golf Course
38890 Hodgson Rd.
Willoughby, OH 44090   Phone: 953-4280

Manager: Gordon Haworth

18 holes
Tees	Yds.	Course	Slope
Middle:	6095	67.8	110
Back:	6440	69.4	113
Forward:	5700	70.9	112

Season:	year-round
Hours:	sunrise–sunset
Greens fees:	$6.50 / $12.00 wkdays; $7.50 / $14.00 wkends
Special rates:	seniors: $1.00 off 9 holes, $2.00 off 18 holes; same discount on carts
Carts:	$9.00 / $16.00
Tee times:	required wkends and holidays until noon
Practice facilities:	range, practice green
Clubhouse facilities:	food, beer, wine; two pavilions with grills
Outings:	catered daily
League play:	wkdays 4:00–6:00 p.m.
Pro shop:	lightly stocked
Lessons:	group and private lessons available, various rates & times
Ranger:	daily

Manakiki Public Golf Course
Willoughby Hills

It is more than rumor: Cleveland Metroparks management plans to rebuild the 8th tee at Manakiki and bring it back to its original site, behind the seventh green.

Donald J. Ross, the Scotsman from Dornoch, designed the course in 1928. (Ross apprenticed at St. Andrews under Old Tom Morris—the father to Young Tom Morris, but no relation to Big Tom Morris, current Metroparks manager of golf operations.) No. 8 was—and is—the number one handicap. With the original tee restored, however, it will be one of the toughest par 4s in the area.

The course was originally a private club but given to the park board in 1962. Mary Lou Colbow (of Black Brook Country Club) dispels the myth of Howard Metzenbaum securing the club for the public. No, Mrs. Colbow said, the owners, Jim and Fanny Brown, wanted to give it to the city of Cleveland—which already had 72 holes between Highland and Seneca—but then-Mayor Lausche had no use for it. They offered it to the park board, now Metroparks, which leased it for 99 years with the lease renewable every year. A thank-you note to the Browns, on a brass plaque, is mounted on a huge stone in front of the clubhouse.

Manakiki has turned into one of the premier public courses in the area. A great deal of work has been completed in recent years and more is planned for the immediate future. A watering system is in place, cart paths have been built, and the tee at No. 13 is completely rebuilt. One hopes the budget will allow for markers at the tee providing hole number and length.

Many area companies hold their outings here. In addition to a first-rate course, the club has a ballroom and a caterer of long standing. Many foursomes finishing the last hole on Saturday afternoons climb the last few yards from the green and see newlyweds posing for wedding pictures while a reception awaits in the ballroom.

Tee times are in order for weekend play and a call to check the outing board is always a good idea. The course looks better now than it has looked in a long time, though it never looked bad. One reason is Joe Klein, who hired on a few years ago as greenskeeper.

The first hole is the only homely one on the course. A 375-yard par 4, it begins with a blind tee shot up a wide fairway. To the left front of the tee is the practice green; the practice range (available for a dollar) is to the right. A line of pines separates fairway from range, which is not o.b. About 170 yards from the tee is a large trap in the left rough, an easy hazard to find. The rising fairway crests near the 150-yard marker (4 x 4s with easy-to-read numerals—another improvement of recent vintage). There is sand on the right front of the green, which is flat.

No. 3 is one of four terrific par 5s on this layout. The driving area is very generous on the left side, but missing to the right can send the ball over the edge of a valley and into another fairway. Getting back can be difficult. From the tee of this 451-yard hole, the fairway dips and then rises until, about 225 yards from the tee, it drops away into a valley. Water cuts across the bottom of the valley 130 yards from the green. On the other side of the water, the ground rises just as suddenly as it fell, then levels toward the green. This green has a great deal of action in it; a huge dip in the front can make two-putting a monumental task.

To speed play, the course often provides a ranger on this hole. The ranger staff is volunteer, mostly retirees, who get to play in exchange for their service. They are a considerate and understanding lot. They spot balls and offer encouragement.

No. 6, a 533-yard par 5, begins at an elevated tee and bends right into a valley that rises and falls a few times en route to the green. This drive has to be accurate; it is a narrow fairway.

The first two shots are played in the valley, which slopes left toward deep brush and woods. The second shot is blind because the fairway rises considerably near the 150-yard marker. From there it dips and rises to a sizable green with sand on the left as well as behind. The two par 5s on the front side offer all the adventure a player could ask for.

No. 7 is a downhill par 3 of 155 yards. On the right side is plenty of sand and farther right is deep woods and a valley. Woods surround the hole, high on the left side and falling away in the rear. It doesn't seem like a tough hole until you miss the green.

The tee for No. 8 used to be behind this green. The tee shot on this 379-yard par 4 had to get out of the woods and draw down the fairway. Through the fairway lies great trouble: trees, equipment sheds, and uneven terrain. Helping to stop some balls headed that way is a brace of sand traps on the right side. But the tee box was repositioned many years ago and the fairway today lies straight in front. It slopes sharply left, and on the other side of the rough the ground falls away to a water-filled valley. Taking a drop there means an almost-blind shot to the green. There are grass bunkers on the right side close to the sloped green, but no sand. Poor shots, especially from the tee, can be quite costly here.

No. 10 is much longer than it looks. A par 4 of 390 yards, it is the number two handicap hole. It deserves to be. The hole plays from an elevated green into a snake-like valley and then rises at the last 50 yards to a big green. Missing the fairway often means additional strokes. The shaded valley rarely dries out and so provides little roll to drives.

No. 12, the first of two consecutive par 5s, is 465 yards. The hole bends slightly right, then back. It dips into a shallow valley, rises, then drops to valley again. A creek cuts across in the last hundred yards, where the fairway rises to an elevated green. It's a sizable target stuck in the side of a hill. The rough behind it is brutal.

No. 13 is a par 5 of 490 yards or thereabouts. With the new elevated tee on this hole, the unmarked yardage could be 30 yards in either direction. On this open hole it would take a decided slice to reach the tree line on the right. The fairway goes up and down and up to a green protected by sand.

No. 15 calls for extra thought before swinging. It is a 310-yard par 4 that starts left to the 150-yard mark, then drops into a valley. The hole bends back to the right and rises to the green. Missing the fairway to the left sends the ball into deep brush. Missing the fairway to the right puts tall trees between the ball and the green.

No. 17 is a par 4 that looks like a par 5. Though only 401 yards, the first 250 are uphill. When the wide fairway crests, it drops like a roller coaster, hits bottom, and goes straight up to the green. Except for some woods on the right, the problems here are the length and the up-and-down fairway. There is sand at this big flat green.

No. 18 resembles No. 10 because it plays in the same type of narrow, deep valley. At 392 yards its length is similar, too. But this valley is sun-drenched and players getting drives in the fairway have shots to the very small green. Instead of being intimidating, it is an exciting hole. There is water crossing the fairway at 50 yards from the green. From there, the ground rises severely.

The approach shot at 18 is fitting. Manakiki is a dramatic course, marked by great golf history, a wonderful ride over 18 very different holes.

Manakiki Public Golf Course

Manakiki Public Golf Course
35501 Eddy Rd.
Willoughby Hills, OH 44094   Phone: 942-2500

Pro: Jeff Staker

18 holes

Tees	Yds.	Course	Slope
Middle:	6212	70.7	127
Forward:	5762	72.3	121

Season: Mar 18–Nov
Hours: sunrise–sunset
Greens fees: $8.50 / $16.00
Special rates: seniors: $6.50 / $13.00 wkdays only
Carts: $9.00 / $18.00
Tee times: taken, not required; 8 1/2 minutes apart
Practice facilities: putting green, chipping green
Clubhouse facilities: snack bar: food, beer, liquor
Outings: large clubhouse; 3 rooms available
League play: various times
Pro shop: well stocked; Mar 18–Nov 25
Lessons: not available
Ranger: daily
New features: new tee on No. 13; restoring old tees on Nos. 8 and 15; new continuous cart paths

Painesville Country Club
Painesville Township

Much has changed since 1928, when the opening of the Painesville Country Club was featured in *The Telegraph*. A clothing store ad on the same page offered men's suits for $22.50—an extra pair of trousers cost six bucks.

Much remains the same. The course plays and looks just as it did when it opened. It was designed by a Mr. Lamoran, according to old and yellowing news clips. He was the pro at Kirtland Country Club and supervised construction. This layout is a good example of the adage about designers discovering courses rather than building them—it is fitted to the land. The back is tighter than the front and both enjoy dramatic changes in elevation.

The course and stone clubhouse were developed by C.J. Alden, then president of the Painesville Metallic Binding Co. His son, Dick, and grandson, Rich, run them today. The clubhouse has a snack bar and pro shop as well as a large dining room with hand-carved woodwork saved from one of Cleveland's Millionaire's Row mansions. The mantel is easily twelve feet high. On one wall rests a huge moose head. Dick Alden likes to nod toward the beast and say in a confidential tone, "Shot him on the 14th fairway."

The greens fees are among the best values in area golf. And this is the only course offering an all-day ticket. Tee times are taken on weekends and holidays. The course is open all year, but the season for locker rental starts in April and ends in October.

The opening hole is a 521-yard par 5. The tee is elevated and the hole plays first across a shallow valley. The fairway rolls up and down until the 150-yard marker, where it swoops down to the green. Well behind the green is a ravine. There is plenty of sand on this hole—and on this course. Its small greens are of average speed.

It's a walk over the ravine to get to the tee at No. 2, a 394-yard par 4. This was designed as a straight hole, but over the last 50 years a couple of trees near the fairway have grown up and out; they make it look like it bends to the left. As at many of the greens here, mounds surround the putting surface. On this hole, losing the ball to the right or over the green sends it crashing down a ravine. Behind the green is the Grand River. It is at the bottom of a 100-foot cliff and encircles much of the course.

One of many virtues of this course is the dearth of development. There is but a single building visible to players on the round. And when the trees are in foliage, even that structure can't be seen. Play here is quiet, secluded, and beautiful.

No. 3, a 208-yard par 3, is not the longest par 3 on the course. Two on the back side are even longer. A few years after the club opened, the green on this hole was moved 30 or 40 yards to the right. The original position looked good on paper, but too many players sent their balls into an adjacent fairway. The "new" green has sand in front. To the left, the ground slides to a ravine filled with trees. The right and rear of the green are mounds. The putting surface has a great deal of roll to it.

No. 6, a 485-yard par 5, is the birdie hole on this course, according to Rich Alden. It aims right, bends left, and then bends back. There are bunkers, both grass and sand, to contend with near the hole. But the hole's S shape does not have severe angles and is largely open. A mistake here can be corrected without real penalty. .

No. 7 is a 386-yard par 4, a straight hole that rises to the green, 60 yards in front of which sits a grass fairway bunker. On the far right side, the rough grows to 12-15 inches. Near the green a stand of black walnuts lines the left side; there are sand bunkers on that side, too. Mounds behind the green shield one of the tees used on the next hole.

There are two tees on No. 8, the famous "bell hole," to allow faster play. When the course is crowded (or when the original tee box just needs some time to recover from play), the second tee is used and it takes 50 yards off the 181-yard hole. There are two ponds, also, so there is water to clear regardless of the tee used. The green was originally cut in the shape of a bell with the bottom facing the tee. To serve as a clapper, a small evergreen was planted in front of the green. According to old news clips, some members disliked the hazard; others were charmed by it. The shape of the green has changed over the decades, but the doughty evergreen remains. It is substantial but not towering, and clearing it is not difficult.

Ten years ago, the ponds were drained. A heavy rain washed some of the muck away and players the next day looked at a shallow pond filled with golf balls. "Golfers can't resist," Rich Alden said, referring to players who showed up at the turn with black muck to their breastbones. They had eased into the pond, grabbing free golf balls until the bottom gave way and lowered them in three or four feet of mud.

No. 9 is a 340-yard par 4 that seems to wind to the green because of elevated terrain on the left side. But though mowed as a dogleg, it really isn't one. Playing a drive off the side of the hill is common. There is sand in the fairway, in the rough, and at the green. On this hole (and on several others) what is called an "extended approach" is cut before the green. It is cut shorter than fairway grass, taller than greens grass, but longer than the typical apron. It adds a handsome country club touch.

No. 11, a par 3 of 239 yards, has a hundred-foot drop from tee to green. When players draw drivers from their bags on a par 3 tee, few expect birdies and most would gladly settle for par. Heavy trees line both sides and o.b. is on the right. The green was once half the size it is today. And it is not a large green. The right side was then protected by a tall pine. Twenty years ago, a disgruntled golfer slipped in under cover of darkness and chopped it down. Other trees are being taken down around the green (by management) in an effort to let in more air and sunlight.

No. 13 is a 402-yard dogleg left, par 4. It offers the most challenging tee shot on the course. From the elevated tee a big draw is called for. And to give players something extra to think about, two 80-foot trees rise up in the left fairway. Clearing them is not difficult but looks so. Trees and thick woods line the left side. The right side is open for the first hundred yards. This hole suggests that players should come here to play the course, not just to play their games. It is a thoughtful layout.

No. 14 is a par 3 of only 109 yards; it is followed by a par 3 almost twice as long. Each calls for good shotmaking. If the green is missed on the first, forget it. There are water, sand, thick rough, tall trees, mounds, and uneven terrain surrounding the green. No. 15, 211 yards, is lined with trees and falls off steeply to the right. It is very narrow—some smart players shoot for the fairway, not the green.

No. 16 is another hole calling for brains over brawn. Its fairway falls from an elevated tee into a valley. There, it bends left. A couple of accurate iron shots can finish off this 251-yard par 4 without trouble. But experience with the hole helps. The approach shot must be precise, as the fairway suddenly and severely narrows. Behind the green is a 60-foot cliff that offers a wonderful view of the Grand River.

The final two holes are par 5s. No. 17 is 471 yards and bends softly right until the last hundred yards, where it turns more sharply and rises to the green. It is very tightly designed, and four bunkers line the path to the green. Work has begun to remove some of the slope from the fairway, making it more level. The work will not interfere with play. The tee will be moved to create a better shot, straightening as well as lengthening the hole. Oak trees and sand traps at the green slow balls hit with too much enthusiasm.

From the 18th tee, the stone clubhouse is visible in the distance. It is an especially pretty hole during the season, when landing areas are trimmed and separated by rough.

Painesville Country Club is off the beaten path. Although it has provided challenge and delight for the better part of the twentieth century, it is a still largely undiscovered course. Only last year did the club put a sign on Route 84, telling passersby that the public is welcome.

Painesville Country Club
84 Golf Drive
Painesville Township, OH 44077   Phone: 354-3469

Manager: Dick Alden

Tees	Yds.	Course	Slope
Middle:	5956	69.0	120
Forward:	5435	71.3	120

Season: Apr 10–Oct 31
Hours: 7:30 a.m.–sunset; clubhouse closes 11 p.m.
Greens fees: $6.25 / $11.00 wkdays
$6.75 / $12.00 wkends, holidays
Special rates: seniors: $4.25 / $8.50; juniors: $5.25 / $9.50 before 2 p.m. wkdays
season, week rates, family rates
Carts: $8.00 / $16.00
Tee times: taken wkends and holidays
Practice facilities: practice range, putting green
Clubhouse facilities: lockers
Outings: steak roasts
League play: Mon-Fri afternoons; some travelling leagues wkends
Pro shop: lightly stocked
Lessons: $12.00 / half hour, by appointment
Ranger: various times
Other: club rental available
New features: regrading 17th fairway

Pine Brook Golf Club
Grafton

It's hard to say which development in golf has provided the most pleasure for amateurs: cut-proof covers on balls, the space-age materials used for shafts, or the forgiving club head. A case can be made for a development of another kind: the interstate highway system. It allows foursomes to quickly crisscross counties for tee times at courses 40 miles and more from home.

It is Interstate 480 that makes Pine Brook Golf Club easily accessible. The clubhouse at this Grafton course was built in 1884. Of course, it wasn't built as a clubhouse, but as a barn. The course itself is young, having opened in 1964 with nine holes. The second nine was added a few years later. For two consecutive years in the mid-seventies, the Elyria Open was played here, which is noteworthy because the course is known not for its difficulty but for the fun it offers players.

It is compact, beautifully maintained (when there is rain), and indeed fun to play. From the white tees, it is 5,741 yards, par 70. Owner Larry Fink, PGA, suggests playing from the blues for more challenge; they play 6,062 yards. Many players mix a few blue tee holes in with their regular white-tee play.

The greens are well manicured; they may be among the healthiest in northeast Ohio. Flower boxes brighten many of the tees and ice water is usually available at several.

Accuracy is often at a premium here and the first hole is a good example. It is only 305 yards, but this par 4 dips in front of the tee, then caroms up and left. The sharp dogleg is filled with rough and trees on the left and, for big hooks, o.b., too. Out-of-bounds comes into play on nine holes, including the first four, which run along the perimeter of the property.

The front side features three par 3s, three par 4s, and three par 5s. No. 2, a short, 485-yard par 5, tempts big hitters. The green can be had in two, but only by avoiding water, o.b., and trees that protect the green. Plenty of players dreaming of eagles when lining up for their second shots walk away with bogies here. Prudence, perhaps an underrated virtue in public golf, is favored here.

No. 6, the second par 5 on the front side, measures 509 yards. It is a straightaway hole but unreachable in two for the overwhelming majority of golfers. By this hole, the dearth of sand becomes noticeable. Fink is mulling the idea of additional grass bunkers, but not sand.

The number one handicap hole is No. 7, a 445-yard par 4. Getting on in regulation would challenge a professional. And three-quarters of the way down the narrow fairway, a stream cuts across diagonally.

No. 9 is a 490-yard par 5 (502 yards from the blues) that includes a lake on the right and a stream across the fairway. But you can't see either hazard from the tee.

No. 14 is a short par 4, but this 320-yard dogleg left tempts almost everyone to sail over the trees in the elbow. Trying but failing often leaves the ball o.b.

No. 16 is another short par 4—335 yards—but it ends with a dogleg right near the green, which is well protected by tall hardwoods.

On No. 18 many players play from the blue tees. Then, instead of a 300-yard par 4 it becomes 345-yards and much more challenging. The fairway slips down and away from the tee then bends left around a lake, rising to an elevated green sitting in the shade of protective trees. A big drive to the right can go through the fairway; a big hook finds the lake and sleeps with the fish.

Fink bought the course only five years ago, having spent almost 30 years as the pro at Wedgewood Country Club. At Pine Brook, he's poured money into the water system (which now has irrigation in front of many greens, eliminating balls

Pine Brook Golf Club

bouncing on hard ground and sailing over the green). The driving range opened last year and new concrete cart paths are being poured. The specialty here is steak dinner outings. The cooking is done by Fink's son and general manager, Terry Fink, who prepped by owning his own successful restaurant in downtown Cleveland.

The senior Fink describes his course as "the type you can play in three and a half, maybe four hours. You can make some pars and birdies. You can have fun."

Pine Brook Golf Club
11043 N. Durkee
North Eaton, OH 44044   Phone: 236-8689 Cleve.; 748-2939 Elyria

Owner: Larry Fink, PGA
Manager: Terry Fink

18 holes

Tees	Yds.	Course	Slope
Middle:	5741	66.8	110
Back:	6062	68.3	113
Forward:	5225	68.9	109

Season: year-round
Hours: 6:00 a.m.–9:30 p.m. summer
9:00 a.m.–5:00 p.m. winter
Greens fees: $6.75 / $11.50 wkdays; $8.00 / $14.50 wkends
Special rates: seniors: $14.00 per person w/cart, wkdays
wkday special: $16.00 per person w/cart
Carts: $9.00 / $18.00
Tee times: not taken
Practice facilities: range, putting green, chipping green
Clubhouse facilities: food, beer; private rooms; pavilion
Outings: enclosed pavilion, 185-person seating
League play: Mon–Fri
Pro shop: lightly stocked
Lessons: by appointment
Ranger: most weekends
New features: new driving range, putting green

Pine Hills Country Club
Hinckley

There is no shortage of area players who argue that Pines Hills is the best public course in northeast Ohio. There is plenty of competition for that mythical title, of course, but little doubt Pine Hills would be a contender. It is not the toughest course, but it is a beautiful and demanding layout. A golf course for people who love to golf. Beginners and slow-pokes are not welcomed.

It is not an old course. Built in 1957, it was designed by Harold Paddock, Sr. Bob Alton, PGA, provides lessons. There is a big and tricky practice green in the front of the clubhouse and on the north side of the parking lot is a huge range that may be used by anyone with a greens fee ticket.

The course record belongs to Joe Kruczek, who shot a 63 from the blue tees in 1989. It is tough to score well here without being adept with long irons and the putter. Kruczek's score is an eye-opener and his record will likely stand for a while.

Pine Hills is not a tight course, but compact. And it is often hilly. The rough is not very rough: 1 1/2". The fairway is kept to a professional 3/4" inch and the greens are trimmed to a fast 3/16".

While it is always wise to get a tee time before setting out, getting one on weekend mornings is impossible. Permanent tee times belong to players who hold them more dearly than chili recipes or directions to a secret fishing hole. "Four guys have to die for one to open up," Alton said.

From the well-stocked pro shop, it's a bit of a walk to the 1st tee, where begins a 333-yard par 4. It's a dogleg right with a lake down part of the right side. The fairway rises slightly toward the green. In the elbow is a sand trap and along the left side, a line of pines. It is not a wide fairway, so accuracy from the tee is at a premium. The green is elevated and has sand on the right front.

No. 3 is a signature hole, though short—a par 4 of only 295 yards. Two nice iron shots can hit the green on this dogleg right. Anything less than that can easily mean double bogey. The first half of the hole is a valley that begins at the tee and ends at the dogleg. From the tee, it's easy to hit through the fairway and reach the woods. To try the corner and come up short means the ball will roll downhill into thick woods. The green is sloped forward and has a trap on the right front.

A climb out of the valley leads to No. 5, where a blind tee shot begins a 471-yard par 5. The fairway rises steadily in front of the tee and bends just a bit to the left. On the right side of the fairway, about 200 yards from the tee, sits a fairway trap. There is more sand at the green. Nos. 5, 6, and 7 play parallel, but each is different.

No. 6 is one of the prettiest tee boxes here. It's a straight par 4, 411 yards long, and it rises and falls—mostly falls—getting to the green. A line of trees runs down the left side and a deep forest is on the right. One of many dangerous greens on the course is found here. It is fairly large and pitched forward. Three-putting is made simple on greens like this.

No. 7 is the other par 5 on this side and, like No. 5, which plays to the left of it, is a blind tee shot. A stepladder at the tee provides a view of players ahead taking their second shots. The fairway on this 467-yard hole rises and slopes to the right. It parts company with No. 5 and goes its own way. Missing the fairway to the right sends the ball into a deep valley. About 175 yards from the green, the fairway suddenly drops, becoming part of the valley that lines the right side. The left side fills with trees and thick bushes. The valley bottoms out, then rises quickly and left to the green. It is not easy to hit in regulation or to hold. A player could shoot this hole six days in a row and play it differently and well each day.

No. 8 is a long par 3 and tough. Between the tee and the green is 195 yards of valley. The green has sand on the right. It is all carry, of course, but hitting too far is more troublesome than hitting short. The rear of the green falls down and away into woods.

No. 10 is a par 5 that starts and ends on high ground but is played in a valley. The left side of the fairway rises steeply and the right side has a creek running next to it. This fairway is not generous. At 473 yards, few players are going to reach the green in two. It's small and flat and a difficult target from the valley.

No. 11 offers a difficult tee shot. That's just one reason why it's the number three handicap hole. A valley sits in front of the tee on this 355-yard par 4. Deep, but not wide, it climbs quickly to a narrow fairway edged by trees, water, and deep rough. Missing the fairway means one thing: trouble. Even hitting the fairway is no guarantee—there are some sand traps and tall hardwoods on the right side of the fairway, both within range of decent drivers.

At the No. 12 tee, newcomers might ask, is every par 3 over a valley? Yes. And this one covers 177 yards to a green lined with trees and sand, the better to stop balls from landing on a nearby tee.

Either of the next two holes, both par 4s, would make a better scorecard picture than the one currently used. No. 13, 391 yards, has a valley in front of the tee, and rising fairway is all a player can see. It doesn't crest until about the 150-yard marker; at that point, it drops steadily to the green. No. 14 is another valley hole. It falls from the tee, then works its way back up. This time, though, the entire hole is visible. Its 376 yards are not long, but in addition to un-level lies there is sand on the right side of the fairway and water on the left. It is a generous fairway, though, and leads to a generous green.

No. 16 is beautiful in person; as a cover shot on the scorecard, it misses. It's a 162-yard par 3 over a valley into the side of a hill. At the bottom of the valley is a pretty lake. On the

Pine Hills Country Club

left side is an old wooden pedestrian bridge that is a delight to use; the cart path is on the right. The ground behind the green continues to rise, right up to the No. 17 tee.

There, Manager Dave Thomas was playing once with Pine Hills shareholders—it's a par 4, 370-yard hole that plays parallel to No. 2, in the opposite direction. Thomas said one of the members of his foursome hit a high slice off the tee. A player on No. 2 did just the same. Thomas and his group were watching their ball when suddenly—click! The two balls hit and dropped straight down. "Think of the odds," he said.

No. 18, a 420-yard par 4, has the potential to create heroes and break hearts. It begins with a pretty tee box, flowers on the right and a split rail fence in the rear. On the left side is the backyard of a residential neighbor. Straight out a few hundred yards is a stand of tall pines, a good aiming point. Staying in the fairway is vital on this hole because the approach shot must clear a couple of lakes where the hole turns 10 or 15 degrees to the left. With a decent tee shot, getting over the water can be done with a mid-iron. That is only to get over. But to hit and hold the green calls for a long iron, and the lakes, often home to a few dozen Canada geese, provide a physical as well as psychological barrier. There is only one chance to make this shot. There is sand at the green, a large target that leans down towards the water.

Alton, Thomas, and the players with permanent tee times are fiercely proud of their course. They should be.

Pine Hills Country Club
433 W. 130th St.
Hinckley, OH 44233   Phone: 225-4477

Manager, Pro: Bob Alton

18 holes
Tees   Yds.   Course   Slope
Middle: 6150   69.8   121
Back: 6463   71.2   124
Forward: 5934   74.3   126

Season: Apr 1–Nov 15
Hours: sunrise–sunset
Greens fees ('91): $8.50 / $16.00 wkdays; $9.00 / $17.00 wkends
Special rates: none
Carts: $9.00 / $17.00
Tee times: taken wkends, holidays
Practice facilities: range, putting green, chipping green
Clubhouse facilities: snack bar: food, beer, liquor
Outings: welcomed
League play: Mon–Fri from 4:30 p.m.
Pro shop: well stocked
Lessons: $25.00 per 1/2 hr.; by appointment only
Ranger: daily
Special rules: foursomes only—singles or twosomes will be paired

Pine Valley Golf Club
Wadsworth

Pine Valley is a beautiful little course, tucked away in the farm country of Medina County and accessible from a two-lane blacktop. The Parsons family—Garland, Dorsalene, and son Gary—draw on a great deal of experience in golf course maintenance. For many years, Garland Parsons ran the Goode Park course near Akron. When he left, he purchased land and created the Bath Golf Club on Medina Line Road, which is now being developed for housing.

The Parsons sold Bath in 1978 to Jim McCartney, who was later shot to death by his former wife. The women who take Table One in Pine Valley's small clubhouse still enjoy talking about the murder. They are still surprised at the murder—not that Mr. McCartney suffered an abrupt end, but that it was his ex-wife who put the bullets in him.

When the bulldozers arrived a few years ago to turn McCartney's course into a housing development, the Bath Men's Golf League switched to Pine Valley, resuming the 30-year-old league's relationship with Garland Parsons.

Of her husband and son, Mrs. Parsons says, "They could grow grass on concrete." The father-son combination looks after the course that was built in 1962 and designed by Cliff Deming. About 40,000 rounds are played here every season, and while getting on is easy during weekdays, a call to the course is rarely wasted; 30 leagues call Pine Valley home.

It is not a long course, 6,097 yards and par 72. Water and sand are minimal. The forward tees are well groomed and provide substantial advantage. The greens are manicured but not particularly fast.

There are plenty of pines at Pine Valley (and more going in every year), but they share space with sweet birch, pin oak, ash, dogwood, hickory, and witch hazel. The witch hazel, which blooms in the fall, has forked branches said to divine water in the right hands. If the right hands walk toward the area between the fifth, sixth, and seventh greens, water will surely be found—there is a large pond there. The additional pines being planted are going in to provide both guidance on holes and protection from errant shots.

No. 1 is Gary Parsons' favorite hole. Because, he said, it's the prettiest. It is indeed one of many pretty holes here. Not only the trees that line almost every fairway, but the gently rolling farmland of this deep green course make it a beautiful layout to walk and play.

The opening hole is a straight par 4 of 416 yards. No. 2 is shorter, only 376 yards, and this par 4 bends slightly left. No. 3 is a par 3 and, at 192 yards, a long one.

Two rules help quicken play here: the continuous putting rule (unless the ball or your feet interfere with another player's line, you're obligated to putt out), and the stand-aside rule (which calls for waving the next group up on par 3s).

No. 4 is a 496-yard par 5, a simple and straightaway hole. No. 5 plays parallel to No. 4 but is only a 409-yard par 4. Halfway to the green it bends to the right. Behind the green is the pond, though here it should not come into play. No. 6, a par 3 of 164 yards, has the pond on its right. No. 7 is a short par 4, 271 yards. Fairway sand on the right side in front of the green adds a little difficulty and the pond here patiently waits for the big shank.

Nos. 8 and 9 make their way back to the clubhouse, the former a short par 5 of 476 yards, the latter a short par 4 of 255 uphill yards.

The back side starts with a 331-yard par 4, a hole with traps in the fairway and at the green. The tee at No. 15, a 363-yard par 4, provides one of the most scenic views on the course. The right side here is lined with old hardwoods. At No. 17, another long par 3, the terrain is up and down getting to the green. For its length—212 yards—3-woods and 4-woods are often used. The finishing hole is a 471-yard par 5 that rises for

Pine Valley Golf Club

the first 200 yards and then suddenly turns left. Before it can get to the green, the fairway drops to a valley, then rises again.

A trip to Pine Valley is not made by those hungry for heroic shots and exciting play. The course is peaceful and fun—plenty of opportunities for pars and even a few birdies. It is easily accessible and offers good value. And if players are fortunate enough to sit in the clubhouse within earshot of Mrs. Parson's friends, the entertainment is first rate, too.

Pine Valley Golf Club
469 Reimer Rd.
Wadsworth, OH 44281   Phone: 335-3375

Owner: Garland Parsons

18 holes

Tees	Yds.	Course	Slope
Middle:	6097	n/r	n/r
Forward:	5268	n/r	n/r

Season: Mar–Nov
Hours: 7:00 a.m.–sunset
Greens fees: $7.00 / $12.00 wkdays; $8.50 / $15.00 wkends
Special rates: seniors: $5.50 / $8.50 wkdays before noon
Carts: $8.50 / $17.00
Tee times: required
Practice facilities: putting green
Clubhouse facilities: food, beer
Outings: available for small groups
League play: wkdays
Pro shop: lightly stocked
Lessons: not available
Ranger: none

Pleasant Hill Golf Course
Chardon

Sue Bania manages this 27-hole layout for owner and builder Tucker Pfouts. His layout has a few doglegs, a few hills, and some water. Many of the fairways here are wide and tempting. Sand is used judiciously and the greens are kept in very good condition. It is a lovely course, and a good one to walk. Very playable, too, and many golfers finishing on the 18th green succumb to the temptation of another, fresh nine holes.

The first hole is a wide open par 4 of 390 yards. Trees line the right side and there is forest behind the green. A few pines dot the left side, and there is sand on the right side of the green, but this is a hole to par and get the game off to a good start. No. 2 is shorter, at 347 yards, but this straightaway par 4 calls for more accurate shotmaking. It is a narrow hole with a water-lined valley about 175 yards from the green. Deep woods line the whole right side and, closer to the green, woods edge the left.

No. 4 starts the climb back up and out of the valley. A 323-yard par 4, it has a generous fairway and equally generous green. The view from this green, looking over the valley, is quite pretty.

No. 6, a long par 5 of 560 yards, is lined on the right side with woods. Just in front of the tee is a small lake with cattails filling the far shore. There are trees on the left side as well, but not so thick as to hide balls. The trees separate this fairway from the 9th fairway. This is a good birdie hole. Days probably go by without anyone getting on in two, but it's not difficult to get on in regulation and there are no hazards in the way of the approach shot.

No. 8 is a 223-yard par 3, the sort of hole that gives bragging rights to players getting on in regulation. It plays over a wide valley and has no sand at the green. No. 9 is another long one, a par 5 of 603 yards. Reaching in four is no shame here. There is some water on the left side, the little lake that sits on the front of the 6th tee, but it is not a concern for straight hitters.

The back side begins with a 535-yard par 5 that climbs. The last 150 yards are marked by a decided leftward tilt. It is comfortably wide. The green is slightly elevated but has no sand. No. 11's scenic tee looks out over a shallow valley with lines of hickories defining the hole. This par 4 is 369 yards to a bunker-free green.

No. 13 is a 382-yard par 4 played in the corner of the course. The tee shot is blind; a transmitter tower in the distance provides a good aiming point. The fairway rises gently all the way to the 150-yard marker, then drops as it bends to the right and to the green. On the left side of the fairway are thick woods and on the right, a line of apple trees.

No. 15, another wide par 4, is 410 yards, with thick trees down the left side and a few on the right. The fairway rises to about the 170-yard mark, then bends right toward the hole. The lake from the previous hole shows up here, waiting on the left side 50 to 100 yards from the green.

No. 16 is a sharp dogleg left, a 350-yard par 4 that has deep woods and a little creek running down the left side. The water cuts across the fairway 50 yards from the green. This hole can be played with irons.

Nos. 17 and 18 are par 3s, the former 165 yards and the latter 204 yards. Both tee shots go over water that should not come into play. No. 18 is the more difficult, not only for the length but because the hole plays uphill.

The third nine starts with a 402-yard par 4 that has a small lake on the right. The lake adds to the beauty of the course but should not add to the score. The left side is filled with hardwoods but the right side is open.

No. 2 is found across Butternut Road. It is a big dogleg right, a 483-yard par 5. In the elbow is a lake. No. 3 is a 391-yard par 4 with a more narrow fairway, one that will penalize slices. The green slopes sharply to the right.

No. 4 is only 106 yards, a par 3 with a green surrounded by hardwoods. No. 5 is a par 3 of more normal length: 172 yards. Woods line the right side and portions of the left.

Back across the road, No. 6 is a 460-yard par 4, a dogleg left with blind tee shot. This is the number three handicap hole and from the women's tee plays 407 yards. There is plenty of room in the fairway on this hole and it leads to a large green. Still, 460 yards is a long, long hole.

No. 7 is just the opposite: a short par 4 of 275 straight yards and a few well-filled sand bunkers between tee and green. No. 8 is another generous and straight fairway, 385 yards long. No. 9 is a par 5 of 485 yards. It rises and bends softly to the right, finishing at a big green.

Tucker Pfouts built a scary roller-coaster course. This is not it. The walk-on-the-wild-side course is nearby Pleasant View. Pleasant Hill is a very nice stroll through the woods, a course that doesn't demand golf prowess, only that players stay up with the foursome before them.

But 27 holes in a day is a dream (or a daydream) for a lot of players. Give them tee times, they will come.

Pleasant Hill Golf Course

Pleasant Hill Golf Course
13461 Aquilla Rd.
Chardon, OH 44024   Phone: 286-9961; 285-2428

Manager: Sue Bania

27 holes	Front & Middle 9s			Front & Back 9s		
Tees	Yds.	Course	Slope	Yds.	Course	Slope
Middle:	6329	n/r	n/r	6295	n/r	n/r
Forward:	5447	n/r	n/r	5836	n/r	n/r

	Middle & Back 9s		
Tees	Yds.	Course	Slope
Middle:	6352	n/r	n/r
Forward:	5599	n/r	n/r

Season:	Apr–Nov/Dec
Hours:	sunrise–sunset
Greens fees:	$6.00 / $10.00 wkdays; $6.50 / $12.00 wkends
Special rates:	wkdays: 27 holes, cart, lunch for $22.00
	seniors: $5.00 / $8.00 wkdays
Carts:	$9.00 / $16.50
Tee times:	not required, suggested for wkends
Practice facilities:	range, putting green
Clubhouse facilities:	snack bar: food, beer; banquet facilities to 300
Outings:	specialize in outings
League play:	every evening 5:00–6:00 p.m.
Pro shop:	well stocked
Lessons:	by arrangement
Ranger:	wkends, outings

Pleasant Valley Country Club
Medina

This 22-year-old course was designed by Jack Kidwell, who also designed Punderson. Pleasant Valley is a challenging layout rolling through the Medina County farmland. It presents holes that reward thinking golfers and penalize the careless.

It is all golf here. There is no driving range and no lessons are offered. There are no price specials and outings are discouraged. The pro shop has little more than the basics. But for golfers seeking to test their skills, Pleasant Valley offers a great deal.

It's a long course: 6,429 yards, par 72 from the whites; 6,912 and still par 72 from the blues. And it's a mix: tough and challenging holes along with straight and generous ones. The rolling terrain, the water, the wealth of old and sturdy hardwoods provide the setting. The layout takes advantage of each virtue and presents a course for the thinking player.

Fairways are trimmed to 3/4" and the rough is only 1 3/4". The greens are beautiful and trimmed to 1/4". Women are welcomed here and provided a 1,500-yard advantage. During the week, Pleasant Valley can be played in fewer than four hours. For weekend play, add an hour. Owner Bill Ostman knows the course record, 67, but not who set it.

Play begins on a 398-yard par 4 that bends to the left halfway out. It is lined with pines and includes a grass bunker on the left side of the fairway. A white ashs stand guard at the green.

At No. 4, the course begins to show its personality. A 153-yard par 3 sounds easy, but this is not an easy hole to play. It is uphill, for starters, which makes club selection more important. Dense woods fill both sides and a trap waits before the green. At No. 5, a small lake sits next to the tee where a weeping willow moves slowly with the wind. It's not unusual to find ducks paddling back and forth in the lake, especially early in the season, when ducklings abound. The fairway rolls a bit to another small lake, this one in front of the green. A bridge leads the way.

No. 9, the number one handicap hole, is a 575-yard par 5 where much depends on the tee shot. It's an intimidating-looking hole; hardwoods on both sides of the fairway insist on an accurate drive. The fairway bends left, then back to the right as it makes its way uphill to a crest. Trees direct the player as the fairway rises and dips.

The clubhouse, a big and serviceable building, is distinctive for its mansard roof. It is passed en route to the 10th tee. No. 10, a 391-yard par 4, calls for a big drive to the right side of the fairway. At the 150-yard marker, the fairway turns left and drops to the green. All along the left side, from 200 yards and in, hardwoods line the hole.

No. 12 is a beautiful hole, a 384-yard par 4 that features a great stand of old and tall hardwoods. No. 13 is a par 5 of only 456 yards that runs along the edge of the course. No. 14 is a 140-yard par 3. The tree-lined fairway falls down to the green where there is a small lake on the right side. It's not a wide green, but it is 90 feet long.

Nos. 16, 17, and 18 circle a lake. No. 16 is another par 5, 488 yards, and looks more difficult than it plays. The left side of the hole runs alongside Hamilton Road. First the fairway rises slightly, then it drops dramatically to a rough valley, through which runs a small stream. The hole bends to the right and rises to the green which, though it has little sand, is elevated; the sides fall steeply.

No. 17 is a 180-yard par 3 across a steep valley. The big lake being circled here is on the right but does not come into play. Instead, at the bottom of the valley is another, smaller lake. This hole calls for nerve and a good swing.

The finishing hole, a 350-yard par 4, has the lake on the right side much of the way. The fairway bends sharply right; approach shots often have to carry the water's edge. That approach often adds great drama and decides winners.

Pleasant Valley is a handsome and well-maintained course. Of course it's handsome—this is Medina County horse country. Good golf course management and rural beauty can coexist very peacefully.

Pleasant Valley Country Club
3830 Hamilton Rd.
Medina, OH 44256   Phone: 225-2510

Manager: Bill Ostman

Tees	Yds.	Course	Slope
Middle:	6429	70.1	117
Back:	6912	72.3	121
Forward:	4984	67.3	105

Season: Apr–Nov
Hours: sunrise–sunset
Greens fees (91): $8.00 / $16.00 wkdays; $9.00 / $18.00 wkends
Special rates: seniors: $1.00 off, wkdays only
Carts: $8.50 / $17.00
Tee times: taken wkends
Practice facilities: putting green
Clubhouse facilities: snack bar
Outings: not available
League play: Mon–Fri evenings
Pro shop: lightly stocked
Lessons: not available
Ranger: various times

Pleasant View Golf Course
Newbury Township

Tucker Pfouts warmed up by building Pleasant Hill, 27 holes in nearby Chardon. Having refined his ideas about a tough golf course, he built Pleasant View.

He is not done building, though the course is essentially complete. Still missing are amenities such as clubhouse, pro shop, practice green, and driving range. Outings are not held here, and there is no league play. Not yet. The course opened in the early spring of 1991.

It is a fascinating hilly ride through dense and beautiful woods, a course where nothing is more important than accuracy. Accuracy and extra balls. Even the best players are going to lose one or two on this tight layout. One of the local rules limits searches to 3 minutes.

No. 1 is a 330-yard par 4 that bends first left, then back to the right. No sense in trying to cut the corner, which is filled with tall trees. The fairway is hilly and mounds line the last few yards to the green. Missing this green means three minutes in deep woods.

No. 2, a 355-yard downhill par 4, is another dogleg, though this time to the left. Tall, tall trees line the right side of the fairway and slicing here courts trouble.

No. 4, a stunning 495-yard par 5, twists, rises, and falls. Much of the way it is lined with old and beautiful trees. There is water on the left and a big, sand-free green surrounded by mounds. Standing on the green, players can look back toward the tee, take in the indescribable fairway and wonder, "I just played that fairway?"

No. 6 tee calls for an accurate long iron. It is a 179-yard par 3 but all downhill. If a draw becomes a hook, a lake at the left of the green waits to swallow the mistake.

On No. 8 the fairway again moves a bit—up and down here. A 328-yard par 4, the two valleys on the way to the green are remarkably deep. The hole is not tight but is made difficult by the steepness of the valleys. The green has more mounds around it and falls off steeply on the left side and the rear. No. 9 is another two-valley hole, a 498-yard par 5. It is about 200 yards out to a dogleg left; the turn is filled with maples.

There is little to slow players at the turn, although soft drinks and beer are available. No. 10, a par 4 of 355 yards, is a downhill hole that bends a bit to the left. At this point, players should check their watches. Finding their way back to the clubhouse in daylight is not easy; with the sun down, these hills can be confusing.

No. 11, a 382-yard par 4, begins at an elevated tee. The fairway goes out a hundred yards with hardwoods on both sides, then drops. There is water to clear with the approach shot; a lake is draped across the fairway. On No. 12, the water is in front of the tee. Almost halfway out, this 495-yard par 5 turns sharply right. The fairway is narrowed by trees, but the green is sizable.

The final three holes are short- and mid-length par 4s. No. 16, a 333-yard uphill dogleg left, is a trying hole. Just a hundred yards out in the left rough is a stand of tall tress. Near the 150-yard marker, the fairway makes its sharp turn and eases into a valley, where the green is found surrounded by trees. No. 17 is a 382-yard dogleg right with a narrow landing area. No. 18, only 298 yards, has a huge crease down the middle of the fairway. In the approach, the fairway narrows to ten yards across.

Pleasant View is a rough and fun course, but one that must be played a few times to get a feel for it. It was chopped out of hilly woods and assumes players can make a ball follow directions. Walking it is a workout, unless with Sunday bags. For those who opt for riding carts, a word of caution: pay attention. The turns come quickly.

Pleasant View Golf Course

Pleasant View Golf Course
14085 Ravenna Rd.
Newbury Township, OH 44024   Phone: 286-9961

Manager:	Sue Bania

Tees	Ydg.	Course	Slope
Middle:	6100	n/r	n/r
Forward:	4980	n/r	n/r

Season:	Apr 15–Oct 15
Hours:	sunrise–sunset
Greens fees:	$6.00 / $10.00 wkdays, $6.50 / $12.00 wkends
Special rates:	$8.00 for 18 holes (no cart inlcuded) wkdays
Carts:	$9.00 / $16.50
Tee times:	taken wkends
Practice facilities:	none
Clubhouse facilities:	none
Outings:	not available
League play:	weekdays
Pro shop:	none
Lessons:	not available
Ranger:	wkends
New features:	brand-new course; planning clubhouse, snack bar, and practice facilities

Punderson State Park Golf Course
Newbury

Ohio cities and Ohio counties own and operate golf courses, so why not the state? The Department of Natural Resources, in addition to scraping road kills off park roads, runs a beautiful golf course designed by Jack Kidwell and built in the spring of 1969. Greens fees, given the course and the condition in which it is kept, are a steal, and well worth the drive.

Course and park are named after Lemuel Punderson, the first permanent settler of Newbury. He worked during the latter part of the nineteenth century for the Connecticut Land Company. A direct descendant with the same name still lives in Newbury.

It is a lot of golf course: 6,600 yards, par 72. But that doesn't mean a slew of lengthy par 4s. Much of the yardage comes from the par 5s; four of them total 2,158 yards. And both par 3s on the back side measure close to 200 yards.

While the ability to hit a long ball is an asset here, more important are the mid- and short-games. Greens are kept at a near-bald 1/8", fairways at 9/16", and the rough allowed to bloom to 1 1/2". The season at Punderson runs from the first of April to the first of November. Outings are available, and special packages that include lodging in the Manor House or the cabins are delightful mini-vacations.

The clubhouse looks more like a ski lodge and has a large porch from which to sip a post-round beer, admire Mother Nature's woods, and watch players on the first tee.

No. 1 is a 371-yard par 4 with heavy woods on the right and a thin line of trees on the left. The fairway dips at the 150-yard marker and turns right as it gently rises toward the green.

There is plenty of sand at the green, which is marked by big, gentle rolls.

No. 2 is another par 4, 364 yards of generous fairway that rises to a crest about a hundred yards from the green. This green has steep sides; hitting them will send a ball 30 or 40 yards from the target.

No. 3 is the first of the big par 5s—this one 550 yards. The fairway is beautiful from the tee. The hole plays straight, but the greenskeeper, with light mower, puts a wavy edge on the right side of the fairway and a straight edge on the left. Out on the left is a huge and ancient willow. There is water farther to the left. (It belongs to another hole and unless a powerful snap hook is in a player's bag, it should not come into play.) There are hills and dales in this green, and four traps around its borders. Behind it is the next tee.

No. 4 is a straight 393-yard par 4. It is the third consecutive hole along the boundary of the course and has o.b. on the right. The fairway is wide, and the green has plenty of sand.

No. 6, another 550-yard par 5, has a small lake in front of the tee. It is an open fairway for the first 200 yards before trees appear on the edges. The first two shots here are blind because the slowly rising fairway doesn't crest until the 150-yard marker. This green is under heavy guard of sand.

No. 8, the number one handicap hole, demands an excellent shot from the tee. The par 4 is 411 yards and the narrow fairway is lined with trees as it bends to the right. A big soft fade is the first step toward par on this hole. A big soft draw can bounce into deep woods on the left. The approach shot has to clear a pond that sits in front of the green. The green itself has plenty of sand. A hole to play with care.

No. 9 is a 164-yard par 3, a shot that has to sail past the stand of pines on the left and hold the green instead of skipping into sand or more pines behind the green. The water from the last hole is on the right but should be difficult to hit.

The snack bar between the 9th green and the 10th tee is a convenient stop for refreshment. No. 10 is a 330-yard par 4.

Stands of hickories and maples underscore the importance of keeping the ball in the fairway. It rises until the 150-yard marker, where the hole turns sharply right. It opens after the dogleg and the green has sand only on one side.

No. 11, a 390-yard par 4, is a magnificent hole. It is open but calls for an approach shot to clear a lake before the green. The lake is substantial and anchored on both sides by willows. This is another hole that gives pause to players when they stop to appreciate the fairways sculptured with light mowers.

The tee shot on No. 14, a 196-yard par 3, has to clear water covering much of the fairway and hold the green. There is fairway in front of the green for players unable to hit that shot. Among Punderson's many virtues are the challenging par 3s. None is easy; all are gorgeous.

No. 15, a 571-yard par 5, has a green unreachable without three very good shots. Deep woods line the right side, though that should not present problems because of a generous fairway here. A deep narrow valley opens up about 200 yards from the green. The valley is rough and cuts across the fairway. The second section of fairway picks up and heads straight to the green.

No. 17 is a 402-yard dogleg right. First-time players will look down the fairway at a lake in the distance and think the hole continues over the lake. It doesn't. The fairway takes a right and heads for the green, the water becoming a hazard on the left side of the fairway.

No. 18 is a 487-yard par 5, a straightforward hole with young trees on both sides. As the years pass, these will make it more narrow. The tough approach shot includes big sand traps that lie around the green.

Punderson doesn't get the play it might if more players realized the value there. It is a first-class course and easy to get to. Greens fees are scandalously low and the staff is helpful and professional.

Judging by this course, the county courses, and many of the muni courses, it appears that government may finally have stumbled on something it can do well.

Punderson State Park Golf Course

Punderson State Park Golf Course
11755 Kinsman Rd. (at Rtes. 87 & 44)
Newbury, OH 44065   Phone: 564-5465

Superintendent: Chip Manyo

Tees	Yds.	Course	Slope
Middle:	6600	72.0	114
Back:	6815	72.9	119

Season: Mar–Nov
Hours: sunrise–sunset
Greens fees (91): $6.00 / $10.00 wkdays
                         $7.50 / $14.00 wkends
Special rates: n/a
Carts: $11.00 / $19.00
Tee times: wkends (taken starting preceding Thu)
Practice facilities: putting green, practice area
Clubhouse facilities: snack bar, large porch
Outings: available
League play: some
Pro shop: lightly stocked
Lessons: new pro this year; to be determined
Ranger: various times
Other: guests at lodge get preferential tee times
New features: work continues on drainage system

Ridge Top Golf Course
Medina

There are only two types of golfers, according to owner Bob Emery: considerate and inconsiderate. "Fifty percent of your golfers will repair the greens where the others will not." That is important to Emery, who said, "The greatest thing about our course is its country club–style greens." Like many other owner/operators, he takes great pride in those layered sand-and-soil gardens so fragile, yet so important to the game.

Ridge Top was Medina County farmland 25 years ago. Across Tower Road is a farm; its silo provides an aiming point on one of the tees. The course was designed by Bob Pennington and plays 5,893 yards, par 71.

Emery constantly evaluates the playability of his course and last year radically changed No. 11 from a short and straight par 4 to a lengthier dogleg. Regrettably, he is no longer able to trust Mother Nature to provide enough rain in a timely manner and so has begun putting in irrigation lines.

Many leagues play at Ridge Top and the outing business thrives. There is no driving range, but a putting green replicates what will be found on the course.

The front side, 3,030 yards and par 36, is much more interesting than the back side. It starts with a 360-yard par 4 that is not, despite its length, an easy warmup hole. White o.b. stakes line the right side and on the left the terrain drops to a valley where the next hole is played. The fairway is not narrow, though, and a decent drive (one that misses the big oak on the right edge of the fairway at the 150-yard marker) will suffice. Overshooting the green will send the ball into deep rough and nearly off the course. These greens are fast.

No. 2, the par 3 in the valley, is the number one handicap hole. The tee and the fairway are in the valley—missing right or left can be troublesome—but the green is steeply elevated. Tall shrubs line the back of the green and protect players on the next tee.

No. 3 is the first of several tough doglegs. It is a 384-yard par 4 with a sharp right turn about 200 yards out. The elbow is filled with trees and uneven ground; only very big hitters will succeed in cutting this corner. After the turn, the hole falls slightly to a narrow creek bed. A few tall trees there can get in the way, but the fairway remains wide as it rises to the green.

No. 4 is the first par 5, only 450 yards and another big dogleg—this time to the left. No fair trying to cut the corner here; it's a long, long shot over short shrubbery and is marked o.b. The wide fairway travels over gentle hills and the right boundary of the hole is also o.b.

The doglegs don't stop yet. No. 5 is only 287 yards, but this par 4 rises from the tee and turns left to get to the green. It's difficult to find a spot to aim at from this tee; this is where the silo in the distance can help. The fairway rolls up and down, finally rising to get to the green.

No. 7 is a beautiful par 5, 485 yards of rolling fairway shored up on the left by a country road. Playing too far right can leave tee shots in fairway sand. The green is big and fast—putting right off it is not difficult. Pin placement can mean a stroke or two here.

The back side begins with one of the more difficult and challenging holes on the course. No. 10 is a 425-yard par 4 that calls for two very good shots. From the tee, players look across a deep valley to the fairway, which bends left and slopes down to the green. All along the right side it is wide open. But all along the left are deep woods. Behind the green are tall hardwoods. It is the number four handicap hole and a real challenge to par.

There is a nasty little gorge just in front of the No. 11 tee, but unless players top the ball it is only decorative. This is the hole just rebuilt by Emery. What used to be a straight par 4 of 230 yards became 90 yards longer when the green was moved. And now it is a dogleg left. The left side has not changed; it is filled with deep woods. The right side is open, though playing to the right only lengthens the approach shot. The green is nestled in thick woods, which were cleared for the hole. It was an expensive change, but one of great value to the course.

No. 12 begins a series of three holes parallel to each other and very similar. All have fast and tricky greens. First, a 460-yard par 5 with a farmer's field—and o.b.—along the left side. To the right is the fairway of No. 13, a 344-yard straight par 4. No. 14 is only 316 yards, but has a lake hiding in the right rough easily reachable from the tee. The fairway tends to slope toward the water.

No. 16 is a 375-yard par 4, but this par 4 is not played on a trouble-free fairway. Leaving the ball left means no chance of getting on in regulation: a big stand of trees leans out and blocks the approach. And on the right is water reachable by big hitters. The approach shot must clear it and stop before sailing into a fairway behind the green.

No. 18 is a delightful par 3 at the edge of a steep hill. Straying here is costly because the woods are deep and thick. And missing the green short or long can send the ball to sleep with the fish. It's a little finesse shot of 122 yards that can easily be the start of a birdie hole. It can also be the start of a bogey—or worse.

Ridge Top is off the beaten path but worth the effort it takes to find. It has a great variety of holes, good prices, and enlightened management. Over the next few seasons, an irrigation system will be installed. Too bad Emery can no longer trust Nature to hydrate his acres of fairway and rough. But players come first here, and they demand healthy grass and greens that hold.

Ridge Top Golf Course

Ridge Top Golf Course
7441 Tower Rd.
Medina, OH 44203   Phone: 725-5500

Owner / Manager: Bob Emery

18 holes

Tees	Yds.	Course	Slope
Middle:	5893	66.8	103
Back:	6211	68.7	107
Forward:	4968	67.3	105

Season:	Mar–Dec
Hours:	sunrise–sunset
Greens fees:	$7.00 / $12.00 wkdays; $7.50 / $14.50 wkends
Special rates:	seniors: $14.00 for 18 holes w/ cart
Carts:	$8.00 / $16.00
Tee times:	taken daily; required wkends
Practice facilities:	putting green
Clubhouse facilities:	food, beer, liquor
Outings:	available to public
League play:	various times
Pro shop:	well stocked
Lessons:	not available
Ranger:	most days
New features:	two enlarged tees; more yardage markers

Ridgewood Golf Club
Parma

There is an ancient oak next to the practice green here and at the base of it a plaque. It is inscribed, "In memory of Howard A. Stahl, 1875-1930. A pioneer in the development of the City of Parma and builder of Ridgewood Golf Course. Erected in his memory by his wife, Agnes Whitmore."

Clearly the course has been around awhile. It has not always been owned and operated by City Hall, however—Parma did not assume ownership until the mid-fifties. By that time, the original layout of the course had been sacrificed for some new homes. Instead of its original 6,306 yards, it now plays 5,825.

Angelo Callari manages the course and keeps copies of the first promotional material produced for Ridgewood. From a brochure written in the mid-twenties:

> Ridgewood is so clean and secluded that one has a feeling of being a long, long way from the city instead of only 20 minutes ride. Because of its character, Ridgewood is ideal to entertain groups of golfing friends or business associates who are frowned upon as guests at private clubs. You can enjoy every facility of the private club, caddies, lockers, showers, good food, iced drinks, etc., at a minimum of expense. Starting times reserved by telephone. Simply phone the clubhouse, LIncoln 3892. Directions by Street Car: West 25th car from Public Square to Car Barns, change to Ridge and Pearl Rd. car, which goes direct to clubhouse.

Stan Schmidt, the starter, remembers many of the early days. He caddied at Ridgewood as a kid. Now 68, he can list

Ridgewood Golf Club

all the holes that were changed or altered for new housing around the course.

Andy Michnay is a little older than Mr. Schmidt and has been playing golf for six decades. In the late thirties, he was playing Ridgewood for ten-cent skins. In those days, the 5th hole ran along W. 54th street and was a 420-yard par 4. "The greenskeeper, Frank Ermer, was moving the hole. Just as he pulled the plug of dirt out for the new hole, my ball bounced in." His playing partners did not protest the eagle.

These days, No. 1 is a 335-yard par 4 wedged in between the 9th and 18th fairways. As the hole makes its way out and left from the tee, it drops a bit, then rises at the 150-yard marker when it bends back to the right. Sand is at both sides of the green. At Ridgewood's tees are well-cared-for flower boxes. The flowers, like the greens, are watered by hand. During dry weather the greens are watered three times a day. This hand-grooming produces healthy greens of average speed.

No. 3 is a par 3, a 170-yard shot over a valley to a green bunkered on both sides. The hole is in a corner of the course and there are homes right next to it. Behind the green and on the left side of the fairway are hardwoods and pines. They provide aesthetic value but also protect homeowners.

No. 5 is a very short par 5, only 435 yards. It's a beautiful hole from the tee, though the green is not visible. The fairway drops off from the tee and rumbles along for a few hundred yards. About 200 yards from the green it begins rising and bending to the right. It's especially easy to measure length on this course because the yardage markers appear to be hewn from telephone poles. They are placed on the edges of the fairway.

No. 6 is a tough, 395-yard par 4. Not only does this hole call for two very good shots to reach the green, but the terrain en route is hilly and hemmed in by trees. When aiming at the green, players must take into consideration a couple of traps.

No. 8 is a brutal par 3 measuring 220 yards and using the creek from the last hole, although the water should not come into play. What will come into play is a forward-sloped green. No. 9, a 359-yard par 4, provides a scenic tee box. After some hilly fairway bordered by hardwoods on both sides, it also provides another place for the creek to meander. This time, the water cuts across the fairway in front of the green.

The first three holes on the back side head toward W. 54th Street, one of the borders of the course. A tunnel under the street leads to the next three holes. The same tunnel leads back for the three finishing holes.

No. 10 is a 365-yard par 4. It begins with a dramatic drop from the tee and an up-and-down fairway bends constantly to the left. A draw off the tee will work well here. Trees stand on both sides of the fairway. The left and rear sides of the small green fall off severely. Missing by just a foot or two can necessitate a pitch of 40 yards back to the green.

No. 12 is a 260-yard par 4 that appears to have been designed by someone walking by and wondering, "where are we going to stick Number 12?" The fairway is lined with trees and rises slightly to a green that appears jacked up 4 or 5 feet. Approaching from the left side puts the ball at odds with a tall tree near the green. There is plenty of sand at the hole.

Then it's back through the W. 54th Street tunnel to No. 13, a brutal and exciting par 5 that covers hill and dale, woods and plain, and 575 yards. The first few hundred yards go straight out from the tee and up. At its crest, the fairway suddenly turns 90 degrees to the right and falls to a green marked by two sand traps on the left and one on the right. The length, the dogleg, and the hills on this hole give bragging rights to any birdie.

No. 15, a 440-yard par 4, runs parallel to W. 54th Street as it makes its way back to the tunnel. Also parallel to the hole is a small creek. Most of the fairways here are generous; playing and staying on the short grass is not as difficult as it is on other public courses.

No. 16 is a 115-yard par 3, uphill to a green well mounded in the back. After par 3s on the front measuring 170, 215, and 220, this hole is a surprise.

Ridgewood Golf Club

No. 17 is a fair distance from the 16th green and is a skimpy 255-yard par 4. The fairway rises the last 70 yards to a wide green. Halfway up to the green is a large sand trap. No. 18 is a 160-yard par 3 to a sloped green with plenty of sand.

Many Ridgewood veterans tell visitors, "You should have seen it before they chopped it up." Such is the price of progress. Even so, Parma is blessed with a good layout that is well run and located in the heart of a crowded city.

Ridgewood Golf Club
6505 Ridge Rd.
Parma, OH 44129   Phone: 888-1057

Manager: Angelo Callari

18 holes

Tees	Yds.	Course	Slope
Middle:	5825	67.9	110
Back:	6299	70.3	115
Forward:	5090	69.1	113

Season: Mar 1–Nov 30
Hours: sunrise–sunset
Greens fees: $7.25/ $12.50 wkdays; $7.75 / $13.00 wkends
Special rates: seniors rates Mon–Fri, restricted hours
                        season pass available
Carts: $9.00 / $16.00
Tee times: not take
Practice facilities: putting green
Clubhouse facilities: snack bar: food, beer, liquor
Outings: available
League play: daily; hours vary
Pro shop: lightly stocked
Lessons: $20.00 per 1/2 hr., Tue–Fri
Ranger: daily
New features: watering system

Riverside Golf Club
Olmsted Falls

Almost 50 years ago, Riverside pro H. Marion Reid was invited to play in the Masters. Unfortunately, the invitation arrived the same day he was supposed to play. And Reed was in the Army. In Panama. It was 1944 and, while he was unable to get to August National, he did win the 1944 Panama Open. Years later his brother Ray presented him with a green jacket. This one, however, bears the Riverside insignia.

Riverside has a lot of golf history. "I think the course was private in the twenties and early thirties," Ray Reid said. He has shares of stock issued in 1928 for the Berea Golf & County Club, the original name of the club. "We nestle in Nature," it reads on the prospectus, a quote from Ralph Waldo Emerson. The club got its current name from the West Branch of the Rocky River. Baker and Robinson Creeks also cut around and through the course.

More unusual than water is the small graveyard that rests next to the fairway on No. 9. Reid calls it the Baker Graveyard for frequent appearance of that name on tombstones there. He guesses an influenza epidemic swept through the area because there are so many headstones for children. The graveyard is o.b.

This designation shows proper respect for the departed. When the 80-year-old Royal Selangor course was first built in Malaysia, the layout included an old Chinese graveyard. Local rules read: "You cannot ground your club in addressing the ball, or move anything, however loose or dead it may be, when you find yourself in a grave."

Riverside is not a long course, 5,498 yards, par 69. But the top three handicap holes are anything but short. It is very walkable. League play has been regular here since the Riverside Golf Association scheduled tee times in 1937. The RGA continues today.

At the first tee is a brass plaque presented to Reid on July 30, 1988. The inscription reads: "In honor of 50 years as our golf professional. Presented by Riverside Women's golf Association." No. 1 is a 363-yard par 4, with a straight and wide fairway. Markers at 150 yards are 4 x 4s and easy to find. Halfway to the cup, on the left side of the fairway, is a huge grass bunker; closer to the green is sand on the left front. The greens here are uniformly good. Ray Reid said, "We don't use sand greens here. We use a third peat, a third dirt, and a third sand." He keeps them trimmed to 3/16".

No. 2 is in the corner of the course. A 309-yard par 4, it begins from an elevated tee and falls into a shallow valley. Trees are a factor on this hole, especially close to the creek that cuts across close to the green. Down the right side is o.b. and a few trees stand in the left rough. But near the water woods grow thick and close in suddenly, making the approach shot more demanding.

No. 3 is an unusual hole, a par 3 of only 101 yards (and depending where the tee is located, often less than 100.) The tee is shaded by an old triple-trunked sycamore. It is virtually a blind tee shot, because ten or fifteen yards in front of the green the terrain suddenly shoots way up. Very little of the green can be seen. There is a large sand trap on the right front and the green leans from back to front. Missing the green short means a steep uphill lie in deep rough, not the average player's favorite shot.

No. 5 is as long as the previous par 3 was short. At 238 yards, few players reach for irons on this tee. All the way down the right side is o.b., and on the left, century hardwoods get in the way of hooked shots. No. 6 is only 49 yards longer, but it's a par 4. It is a straight fairway. The green slopes right and toward a large grass bunker.

A brief walk through the woods leads from the 7th green to the 8th tee. It's a daunting tee, with creek right in front and quickly rising terrain. Hardwoods on both sides define this 330-yard hole. The fairway goes up, stays up, then comes back down. On the plateau, it drops off suddenly on the left side. Trees here can always be a problem. Players unable to keep the ball in play can easily card double bogies and worse.

No. 9 is a 471-yard par 5 that begins with a wide and level fairway. All the way down the right side are deep woods, but to get a ball in there calls for a super slice. After 200 yards, the fairway bends left and the wooded area on the right falls away into a valley. At 120 yards from the green, a large grass bunker sits on the right side of the fairway.

The first two shots on this hole are easy enough and may give rise to thoughts about birdie. But the area in front of the green and the green itself are so littered with ambushes and booby traps that getting away with a par is worthy of note. There are a couple of fairway traps and, at the green, three more traps. Off to the right of the green is the graveyard. (Where lies the body of Uraniam Hickox, who threw off this mortal coil in 1860.) This resting place is o.b. The green itself encourages careful play; one of the penalties easily meted here is putting right off the green. The green is high in back, low in the front. It drops 3 feet very quickly. And it all falls to the right front corner, where a pine tree sits.

The back side here begins and ends with gorgeous par 3s. One in, one over, a valley. No. 10 is 141 yards from an elevated tee to a generous green. The green is on the other side of a creek and is stuck in the corner of the valley. The terrain rises behind it. It's a climb out of the valley to the next tee. No. 11 is a 396-yard par 4 that runs parallel to Sprague Road on the left. There is little excitement to be had on this hole unless a snap hook drive finds the windshield of an oncoming car.

No. 12 is the number one handicap, a long but relatively undistinguished par 4. One hundred yards out on this 430-yard hole sits an Eisenhower tree on the right side of the fairway. Otherwise, it's wide open. On the left side, well beyond the rough, trees and underbrush rise up. But hitting a ball into that trouble is a silent call for help with the game. This hole's length makes it tough and the pin placement can make it much tougher; the right rear portion of the green rises dramatically.

No. 14, the only par 5 on this side, is 473 yards and wide open. This hole resembles the roomy and undefined holes of the Scottish links courses. It bends to the right just slightly and a few trees—not so many that Captain Hook couldn't count them on his fingers—define the shape of the fairway. In the rough on the left side are a pair of grass bunkers.

No. 15 comes back and runs parallel to the previous hole, and this 416-yard par 4 is wide open, too. A stand of hardwoods lines the rear of the green. The length of this hole will prevent many players from reaching the green in regulation. But it is not otherwise difficult and many pars here result from good short games.

No. 18 has all that's needed for a dramatic close: elevated tee, beautiful valley, a stream, elevated green, sand. Only 175 yards, this par 3 inspires players to think and play more carefully than they would on a more usual par 3.

Reid doesn't do much trade in outings and one gets the feeling he is uncomfortable sharing his club with strangers. If time is available, though, players would be well-advised to seek a conversation with him. He carries some great local golf lore and might be willing to share it.

Riverside Golf Club
Sprague & Columbia Rds.
Olmsted Falls, OH 44138   Phone: 235-8006

General Manager: Ray Reid

Tees	Yds.	Course	Slope
Middle:	5498	65.9	106
Forward:	5162	68.9	111

Season:	year-round
Hours:	sunrise–sunset
Greens fees:	$7.25 / $14.50
Special rates:	none
Carts:	$8.00 / $16.00
Tee times:	required daily
Practice facilities:	3 putting & chipping greens
Clubhouse facilities:	food, beer, liquor; banquet facilities; showers & lockers; pavilion
Outings:	company tournaments, banquets, picnics
League play:	daily, various times
Pro shop:	well-stocked
Lessons:	$20.00 per 1/2 hr.
Ranger:	during peak times

Royal Crest Golf Club
Columbia Station

This property has been in the Madak family since the turn of the century. The family farm was developed into a golf course about 25 years ago, the barn into the clubhouse, which seats about three dozen players. Today over 40 leagues call Royal Crest home.

In 1991, construction of cart paths on the front nine was completed and the arbor program was responsible for an additional few dozen saplings, mostly pine, oak, maple, beech, and a few locust. It is a little longer than many area courses: 6,205 yards, par 71. The forward tees don't provide much relief. The numbers one and two handicap holes on the women's course are par 3s measuring 195 and 192 yards; many members of the LPGA might find those holes very, very difficult. The terrain is generally level and the course is well cared for. Clearly, the Madak family plans to keep this course for generations.

The fun begins on a 353-yard par 4 with wide landing area, though o.b. runs down the right side. Trees guide the fairway most of the way to a large, flat green that has no sand. No. 2 is a par 3 that calls for wood at the tee—it's 207 yards, with water down the left side. No. 3 is a straight hole, a par 4 of 345 yards lined with pines. Near the left side of the green a stand of pines separates players from a lake.

The first three holes do not call for heroics (though anyone holding the green on the 207-yard second deserves a round of applause). But they give a good indication of what the course is like: challenging and pretty. On most holes here, you can see what you're going to play. And hitting a long ball is a definite advantage.

No. 4 is the only par 5 on the front side, a 544-yard dogleg left. The hole is played in the corner of the course; much of the right side is o.b. But it's a wide fairway until the last hundred yards. Cutting the corner of the dogleg is impossible. Another tee is near the elbow and the area is marked with white stakes. It also has a stand of tall pines that would challenge even the biggest hitters. This is not a hole for risk-taking. Three good shots will get the ball on the green.

No. 8, a 300-yard par 4 with a huge old birch at the tee, has a surprise; players hooking their tee shots will find the ball at the bottom of a lake unseen from the tee.

The last hole on the front side is pure Royal Crest: long, straight, and lined with trees. No. 9 is a par 4 of 396 yards. The green is slightly elevated and behind it is a sand trap.

No. 11 is not long, but hazardous: a 321-yard par 4 dogleg left with a lake. Hitters who had their Wheaties for breakfast may try the corner. Even after clearing the water, though, the ball can end up behind trees on the left side of the fairway. It's a gamble.

No. 14 is the number two handicap, a 532-yard par 5. Except for a hundred yards of trees going down the right side, it is generously wide. But it bends a bit to the left and in that soft dogleg lies a lake. No. 15 is a tough 433-yard par 4 with a dogleg right. From the tee box, the green is hidden. On reaching it, players find it lined in back with woods.

No. 16 is a fun par 5. Wide fairway and generous landing area tempt players to swing for the long ball. Big hitters not yet in control of their fades, however, might find either drive or second shot o.b. on the right. No. 17 is a par 3, 172 yards, with a tall hardwood on the right side a hundred yards from the tee. The tree is always a strong influence and, depending on pin placement, can dominate the hole. Finishing the round is an easy matter: No. 18 is a 349-yard par 4, pretty and straight.

Royal Crest is a family-run business, first farm, now golf course. The virtues necessary for a successful golf course can't

Royal Crest Golf Club

be that different from those for a successful farm: concern for the land, dedication to customers, and a sharp eye on the future. The Madaks seem to have made the right decision.

Royal Crest Golf Club
23310 Rte. 82
Columbia Station, OH 44028   236-5644

Managers: the Madak family

Tees	Yds.	Course	Slope
Middle:	6205	68.0	108
Back:	6746	70.5	108
Forward:	5903	72.0	112

Season:	Apr 1–Oct 31
Hours:	sunrise–sunset
Greens fees:	$8.00 / $15.00 wkdays; $8.50 / $16.00 wkends
Special rates:	seniors: $7.00 / 13.50 wkdays
Carts:	$7.00 / $13.50
Tee times:	not taken
Practice facilities:	putting green
Clubhouse facilities:	snack bar
Outings:	available for small outings (16–72 players)
League play:	every morning and evening
Pro shop:	lightly stocked
Lessons:	not available
Ranger:	various times
New features:	cart paths on front nine complete; cart paths on back nine being added

Seneca Golf Course
Broadview Heights

Jammed between Valley Parkway and Edgerton Road are 36 holes of golf owned and operated by the City of Cleveland. The city has been in the golf business since the early part of this century. Seneca was built under the Works Progress Administration during the mid-thirties and opened for play in 1940.

Administration of the course, along with sister course Highland, falls today to Edward Rahel, commissioner of urban forestry for the city. Both courses were allowed to deteriorate under various city administrations. Now, Rahel says, they are being run like businesses and he is hopeful for their continued improvement.

Joe Toth is one of the bright spots at Seneca. The chief ranger is one of only three or four paid employees. The rest of the help trade hours at the course for free golf. Most of these men can be found sitting on the park benches outside the clubhouse; what they do is difficult to determine. But when the only compensation is free golf, setting high standards would be foolish. Manager Jennifer Schuyler would not discuss course operations for this book. How a course with volunteer employees and mute management will grow and prosper is unclear.

Too bad management here doesn't take a cue from Toth. The peripatetic ranger-greenskeeper-enforcer clearly enjoys the players as well as the course. As he tours it, his voice rises and falls as he describes hidden hazards, challenging holes, or his own occasional prowess with the sticks.

The B course begins with an easy, 331-yard par 4. It is straightaway and has only a few trees down the left side. In the early sixties, florist John Artale teed off here and rimmed the cup with his drive. As exciting as that shot was, it doesn't top the time he caddied for Sam Snead in the 1938 Cleveland Open, at Oakwood Country Club. Leading by one at the 18th tee on the final day, Snead's drive went right. He asked Artale what he should use to clear a tree and make the green. A seven, Artale said. Snead, overclubbed, sent the ball toward the locker room behind the green. Many balls hit there bounced back in play. But a Cleveland policeman who was providing security opened the door to see what was happening and the ball flew in. Stroke and distance left Snead in second place. He took home $1,500. Less the $40 he gave his caddy for seven days work.

No. 3 is the number one handicap on the B course. The 582-yard par 5 plays along a wide fairway with little trouble on either side. The tee shot is blind, as the terrain rises from the tee. A lake in front of the green is about 40 yards deep and easily 100 yards wide. The B course has only one par 5 and one par 3 per nine.

By this point in the match, one gets used to the groundskeeping. The rough here is not long but often filled with weeds. It has an unkempt look to it. The greens are generally in good shape and well maintained. But the sand traps look as if they were never raked or filled with any new sand.

No. 6 is a 380-yard par 4 that rolls softly downhill toward a lake at the 150-yard marker. Often filled more with mud and cattails than water, the lake is as wide as the fairway. From the other side of the water the fairway rises slightly to a generous green.

Some of the trees on this old course are more than 100 years old and measure 15 to 20 feet around. Many of the holes are defined by trees, but woods don't become a problem except around the perimeter of the course.

No. 9 is only 344 yards, but this par 4 is a tough hole. It's a sharp dogleg left with a rising fairway. In the elbow is a thick stand of tall trees. Along the right side are thick woods and, beyond them, Valley Parkway. Hitting through the fairway is common; the landing area for drives is small. Getting to the elevated green is made more difficult by sand about 30 yards in front and more bunkers and tall trees at its sides.

The front side is unusually long for having no par 4s over 400 yards. The back is longer but has two monster par 4s.

No. 12 is a 477-yard par 5 that begins with a blind tee shot to a fairway that rises for a few hundred yards before bending to the right. Trees line the right side and there is plenty of sand at the green.

No. 13, a 452-yard par 4, is another blind tee shot to a rising fairway. There is a fairway trap on the right and sand on the left side of the green as well. It's a long, long way for the average player to reach in regulation.

No. 15 is a 572-yard par 5 with tall trees lining the first 200 yards. Again this is a blind tee shot, because of the rising terrain, and at the second shot a small lake in front of the green comes into view. The water is about 125 yards from the green. A huge old willow stands at the left side of the water and more trees surround the green, which has sand on its left edge.

No. 16 has a generous fairway, and it should. This par 4 is a long 449-yards to a green with sand on both sides. No. 17 is similar, a wide 375-yard par 4. No. 18 is a 375-yard par 4 with trees on both sides and a troublesome trap 225 yards from the tee on the right side.

All of B Course and the back side of A Course are played in an area east of the clubhouse. The front side of A Course is to the west. Unlike the other three nines, it does not have the wealth of century oaks; it plays a bit more open and is the side used for winter golf.

Sitting between the east and west side of the clubhouse is a practice range and huge practice green. The clubhouse porch overlooks the practice areas and provides a good view of the 18th hole of A Course.

A Course begins with a wide-open par 4 of 362 yards. It

plays a little longer because the terrain rises slightly all the way to the big, bunkered green, but it's a fair warm up.

No. 4 is the first par 3 and it's a pretty one from an elevated tee down to a generous, flat green only 134 yards away. The trap at the right front is edged with railroad ties between sand and green, calling for more lofted shots from the hazard.

No. 6 is a par 4 of 380 yards. The boundary on the left side is Broadview Road. The hole rises slightly; the right side is open. Of importance on this tee is avoiding the sand that juts out on the left side at about the 150-yard marker. There is more sand at the green.

No. 7 is a par 5, a 500-yard dogleg that turns sharply left after a few hundred yards, and drops to a smallish green surrounded by tall trees. The corner is tempting here, but trees fill it and there is plenty of sand to clear.

No. 9 is a tough driving hole, finally. The woods are thick on either side of this 403-yard par 4; it bends to the right about halfway out. Playing the tee shot too far right can make for a very difficult approach. On the left side of the green is sand; behind it is the parking lot and a walk to the 10th tee.

The back side of A Course is the only side here with two par 5s and two par 3s.

No. 11 is a 376-yard par 4 with rolling fairway and beautiful woods (and o.b.) down the entire left side. The woods continue down the left of No. 12, which has a line of trees down the right side as well. It is a 560-yard par 5 with softly rolling fairway but no hazards besides length and sand at the green.

No. 13 is a pretty and challenging par 3, an uphill 154 yards. Woods continue on the left side, as this and the previous two holes play along the edge of the course. Trees can get in the way near the left side of the green here.

No. 17 is awfully long; straightaway 608 yards from tee to green. The fairway is wide and the green only slightly elevated. Except for the length, it's almost hazard-free. But the length of this hole pushes many players to swing much harder than they normally might. The results rarely match the hope. A par on this hole is worth talking about. Just ask Joe Toth how he managed a 5 here.

Seneca has been a part of the services offered by the city for years. That the course suffered at the hands of a few administrations is not a point to be argued. But now, under Commissioner Rahel, Seneca has a more hopeful future. It's possible we'll see it return to proper condition in the coming seasons.

Seneca Golf Course
975 Metro Valley Pkwy.
Broadview Hts, OH 44147   Phone: 526-8033

| Manager: | Jennifer Schuyler |
| Pro: | Renee Powell, LPGA |

36 holes	A Course			B Course		
Tees	Yds.	Course	Slope	Yds.	Course	Slope
Middle:	6588	71.2	118	6691	71.6	121
Forward:	6212	74.6	n/r	6299	75.1	n/r

Season:	year-round
Hours:	6:00 a.m.–8:00 p.m. wkdays
	5:30 a.m.–8:00 p.m. wkends
Greens fees:	$7.00 / $13.00 wkdays; $7.50 / $14.00 wkends
Special rates:	seniors (60+) & juniors: $4.50 / $8.50 Mon–Fri before 3 p.m.
Carts:	$9.00 / $17.00
Tee times:	taken wkends only
Practice facilities:	range area (use own balls), putting green
Clubhouse facilities:	restaurant; liquor license Mon–Sat
Outings:	available; deck area, tent rental
League play:	frequent; 9 holes always available
Pro shop:	well stocked; Mar–Nov
Lessons:	by appointment
Ranger:	daily
Other:	club rental available in pro shop

Shawnee Hills Golf Course
Bedford

Jeff Staker, PGA, will teach the finer (and coarser) points of the golf swing for very good rate. That's but one of the amenities offered at this 32-year-old Cleveland Metroparks course, including: lighted driving range, 40-seat clubhouse, and a four-minute response time from the Bedford Fire Department—especially valuable if players are prone to (or prone from) heart attacks. In addition to the 6,160-yard, par 71 course, Shawnee Hills also offers a 9-hole par 3 layout.

The grounds are very well-tended here. Even driving to the course, if one drives from downtown, is a delight, because the road through Metroparks' Bedford Reservation is filled with beautiful woods, horse trails, picnic spots, and the picturesque Idlevail Falls, where wise newlyweds might pose for wedding photos before changing clothes and heading to the first tee.

No. 1 is a long par 4, 416 yards of wide fairway. The fairway bends a bit to the left and, just before the 150-yard marker, rises slightly.

No. 2 is a 388-yard par 4 and is known around the clubhouse for its narrow fairway. There is inconsequential water just in front of the tee. The fairway rises, levels off, and then dips to the green. Hardwoods add color and potential trouble; woods provide the backdrop at the green.

No. 3 is a 347-yard par 4, another beautiful hole with a fairway that rises and falls a few times before it arrives at the green. Near the 150-yard marker, it falls precipitously and water cuts across at the bottom of the little valley. (Unusual note: this hole is one of three 347-yard holes on the course. A lucky number? The others are No. 5 and No. 15.)

No. 4 is a 470-yard par 5 with fairways wide enough to tempt big hitters to try even bigger. Like much of this course, the fairway rolls between beautiful trees and arrives at a green with little sand. The greens here are uniformly good, and though not noticeably fast, are true.

No. 5 is a 347-yard par 4 with deep woods down the left side. At the tee, old park benches sit beneath maple trees. This is another up-and-down hole, and players overhitting the green will send their balls into deep woods.

No. 9, a 319-yard par 4, is a dogleg left. Cutting the corner here is impossible for most players because of the trees and the length of the shot. The fairway on this hole is quite narrow and opens only a bit after the first hundred yards.

The deep woods are along the perimeter of the course, but the designers of Shawnee Hills kept as many of the old, tall, and stately hardwoods as they could. The trees provide guidance, protection, and hazards. Their stature gives the course a mature look.

The back nine starts next to the driving range. The 364-yard No. 10 is a straight par 4 and its fairway is littered with practice balls. Fortunately, the club uses yellow balls at the range. There is a lake behind this green, but it will have much more influence later.

There is water to contend with on No. 12, a very short par 4, only 271 straightaway yards. A stand of trees shares the right rough with the water, but it is still a tee that tempts players to swing away.

No. 13 is a much longer par 4—at 451 yards, long enough to make trouble. The fairway dips slightly then rises. On the left at that point are huge stands of tall pines. Pines from the same generation line the right side, too. The green is at the end of a slight dogleg left.

No. 16 is the only par 5 on this side, 525-yards. It dips at the tee then rises to the right. The entire left side is filled with pines, and on the right a few trees separate this fairway from the adjacent 17th. The fairway slowly rises to the green.

No. 17 bends left around a long lake. A 377-yard par 4, it may be the best hole on the course. A bumpy fairway follows

Shawnee Hills Golf Course

the lake's edge. There is a stand of pines on the left rear of the green, but no sand.

No. 18 is a wide open, 341-yard par 4. Thin lines of trees go down both sides of the fairway but do not present real obstacles. It is a quiet finishing hole.

But then it's a quiet course. A lovely, simple, and beautifully groomed course that doesn't offer challenges so much as it presents players with the pleasures of the game.

Shawnee Hills Golf Course
18753 Egbert Rd.
Bedford, OH 44146　　　　Phone: 232-7184

Pro:　　　　　　　　　Jeff Staker

18 holes
Tees	Yds.	Course	Slope
Middle:	6160	68.7	112
Forward:	6029	72.5	116

Season:	Mar 18–Nov 25
Hours:	sunrise–sunset
Greens fees:	$7.00 / $13.00; $5.00 par 3
Special rates:	seniors: $5.00 / $10.00 wkdays
Carts:	$8.50 / $17.00
Tee times:	taken, not required
Practice facilities:	range, putting green, chipping green
Clubhouse facilities:	snack bar: food, beer
Outings:	available
League play:	various times
Pro shop:	well stocked
Lessons:	$18.00 per 1/2 hr.
Ranger:	daily
New features:	several new bunkers; snack bar renovation

Skyland Golf Course
Hinckley

Across the street from the clubhouse is a dairy farm, a pastoral reminder of how close rural Ohio still is to Cleveland. Just down the street is an apple and cider market. At the course entrance is a big, blooming flower box built of railroad ties. This is a beautiful and old layout, thought by some to be the oldest course in Medina County.

It brings with it some history. It was the first course in the area, owner Tim Rhodes said, to discard the Women After Eleven a.m. Only rule. "We thought that rule was one of the most arrogant things around. We were the first to break it. We didn't see any sense to it and I have women with permanent tee times on Sunday mornings, as well as women's leagues."

Skyland was built by the father of current operators Tim and Tom Rhodes. The first nine was built in the early thirties and the course was known as Hinckley Golf Course. When the second nine was added, in 1940, the name was changed to Skyland for the views available from some tees. "During the Depression, my mom and dad would charge 25 cents a round. Plenty of people would come out, five and six to a car, and play all day," Tim Rhodes said.

Plenty of people still come out; 30 leagues play at Skyland. The oldest is the Hinckley Skyland Men's League, which first scheduled tee times in 1957. St. Bridget's Holy Name Society started playing in 1960. Both continue today.

The pro shop, a huge and airy brick one-story building, was erected in 1968. A good trade is done in outings. Tee times are available, but permanent weekend tee times are in the grips of long-time regulars. "Some of these go back to 1956, when we first gave out tee times. Even if they move from the area they find a way to move their friends into those tee times so they don't lose the slot."

The front side is much longer than the back. The course plays 3,261 yards, par 37 going out and 2,978, par 35 coming in (only one par 5). Tim Rhodes describes the front side as open and rolling, the back nine as tighter, sportier, and home to the infamous giggly bush. "It's a bush that's very small, but you always wind up behind it and by the time you've finished your round, you've gone beyond screaming and you're giggling."

No. 1 is a par 4, 351 yards, and presents players with a wide fairway, little trouble, and a soft turn of the fairway to the left. This first fairway, like many others here, is softly hilly. It's a hole on which to warm up without courting trouble.

No. 3 is a par 5 with a hilly fairway that is straight and treelined. The tee box on this 480-yard hole is the site of one of the stranger golf stories picked up while researching this book.

A regular foursome, according to Rhodes, was making ready to tee off when one member began complaining about a heart attack. His playing partners accused him of malingering and refused to do anything about his complaints. When he grew more frantic, his partners offered him a deal: they would walk him over to the rough on the adjacent No. 7 and lay him gently down. They would then play holes 4, 5, and 6. When they again reached him on the adjacent No. 7, they would inquire as to his health and, if he still complained about dying, would take him in. So they resumed play as a threesome. A player from another group came across the heart attack victim and, after inquiring how he came to be prone in the rough on No. 7, rushed the man back to the clubhouse and medical assistance.

No. 7 appears short for a par 5, at only 461 yards, but much of the fairway rises, making it play longer than it looks. About halfway out, each side of the fairway is marked with a sand trap. No. 8, a 334-yard par 4, calls for a blind tee shot to a wide and rising fairway that crests about 100 yards from the tee. The fairway slopes left; near the green is a lake on the left. A creek from the lake cuts directly across the fairway. There is a stand of hardwoods in front of the water.

At the turn is a beautiful par 5 of 511 yards. No. 10 is a dogleg left that begins its bend about 200 yards from the tee. Trees define the outer limits of the rough on this wide fairway, and in the last 150 yards or so woods show up on the right, which is also o.b. The fairway dips noticeably then rises to a green with a sand on the right side. The same woods continue down the right side of the next hole.

No. 11 is only 371 yards, but this par 4 has unusual terrain. A thin line of maples and other hardwoods runs down the left side of this straightaway hole. From the tee, the fairway rises slightly, crests, and falls into a valley with a creek running across about 200 yards from the green. The rising fairway then heads towards one of the smallest greens on the course.

No. 12, a par 3 of only 144 yards, can be troublesome as well; it calls for a shot that must carry over a creek and stop on a green backed by woods and o.b. Woods also close in on both sides; the tee shot has no room to wander. To the right of the green stands a 100-foot-tall oak.

The next four holes play parallel to each other. No. 13 also calls for an accurate shot from the tee, which has a ravine directly in front of it. This should not come into play but does add to the physical beauty of the hole. Trees line both sides of the fairway, which rises slightly until about 120 yards from the green. From there it slopes down toward a small lake in front of the green.

No. 14 is a very short par 4, only 286 yards. The last 30 yards, however, fall 25 or 30 feet to a small green. In most cases, it's a blind approach shot.

Players clamber halfway out of the valley to the next tee, where the first shot is blind. No. 15 is a 337-yard par 4 with a wide and hilly fairway lined with thin rows of trees. The green here falls away quickly in the rear and on the sides.

Skyland Golf Course

No. 16 is a 360-yard par 4. The fairway rises directly in front of the tee then slopes down and to the right. Near the 150-yard marker, some new trees have been planted on the left; these will narrow the fairway. Along the right side is a single line of hardwoods.

Skyland is well into its second half-century. It has long offered the golfing public a most wonderful walk in the woods. Management takes care of the big things, such as greens and fairways, and the little things: flower gardens and a warm welcome to the course. Just as it should be.

Skyland Golf Course
2085 Center Rd.
Hinckley, OH 44233   Phone: 225-5698

| Owner / Manager: | Tim Rhodes |
| Owner / Supt.: | Richard Rhodes |

18 holes

Tees	Yds.	Course	Slope
Middle:	6239	68.9	113
Forward:	5563	70.7	112

Season:	Apr–Nov 15
Hours:	7:00 a.m.–sunset
Greens fees:	$8.50 / $16.00 wkends; reduced wkdays
Special rates:	senior discount
Carts:	$8.25 / $16.50
Tee times:	taken; required wkends
Practice facilities:	putting green
Clubhouse facilities:	snack bar: food, beer, liquor; pavilions
Outings:	available for private outings
League play:	heavy Mon–Fri 8:00–9:30 a.m., 4:00–6:15 p.m.
Pro shop:	lightly stocked
Lessons:	not available
Ranger:	most days

Sleepy Hollow Golf Course
Brecksville

One of the toughest tracks in town is Sleepy Hollow, the Cleveland Metroparks course on Brecksville Road. Its ancient clubhouse was recently razed and replaced with a new facility offering amenities not generally seen on public courses: showers, free phones, hair dryers, lockers. At this rate, manager Jim Chambers might soon be offering oil changes and secretarial services.

The course, at 6,335 par 71, is long. The front side has three par 3s and two par 5s. The back side has one of each. Not a course for beginners or players who are easily frustrated, this is a difficult and challenging layout with greens that are among the fastest and trickiest in northeast Ohio public golf.

One more recent change was switching nines. On the old layout, the first hole was a daunting 450-yard par 4 dogleg. Scores on this hole often indicated what would follow for the next 17 holes.

But now No. 1 is a pleasant par 5, slightly downhill the entire length and endowed with a wide fairway. Hitting from the rough is only as difficult as the length of the grass; few trees get in the way of the shot on this hole. Near the green, the right side falls away to a valley and there is sand at and near the green. A tall stand of trees behind the green protects players on the next tee.

No. 2, the Par Three From Hell, is 210 yards to a two-tiered green. Along the right side is a shallow valley filled with dense underbrush and golf balls. The tee is elevated. Once over a small valley in front, the fairway rises slightly. There is sand to the right and left near the green, which is long and rather narrow.

No. 3 is the number one handicap hole on the course, and with good reason. It is a 450-yard par 4, slightly downhill at first before the fairway drops more severely. A big drive has to stay left in order to see the green for the approach. Coming in from the right leaves a couple of tall trees in the way. In front of the green is a small but severe valley. On the left side, deep woods angle in, making the hole more narrow as it progresses. The generous green has sand to the left and right. A tournament hole.

The second par 5 on the front side is a 550-yard hole for big hitters. No. 4 is wide open the first few hundred yards and slightly downhill. At about 180 yards from the green, a couple of tall hardwoods mark the slight bend to the left. For the last 80 yards a valley parallels the hole in the left rough. There are sand traps on both sides near the green.

No. 5 is a 390-yard par 4 that plays longer than marked because it is all uphill. Running along the right side is a creek bed and thick brush. Out a ways and off to the left is a stand of trees. This is not an easy driving hole. The fairway bends to the right toward a generous green protected by sand. On the right about 50 yards before the green is a uniform line of pines. It is pretty but also functional; it protects players on the next tee.

No. 6 is the second par 3 on this side (there are three) and another tough shot. Between the tee and the green is valley; the green sits on a hilltop. Balls missing short can bounce back and down 40 or 50 feet. And there is some sand behind the green to stop balls hit too far. It's a double green here, the second about 20 yards to the right but rarely played.

No. 8, the third par 3 on the front side, is 165 yards to a green protected on the left front by overhanging hardwood branches as well as deep sand. On the right is more sand, then the rough falls away into a ravine. This is clearly not a merciful golf course.

No. 9, a 360-yard par 4, is a blind tee shot up a wide and rising fairway. The fairway crests at about 100 yards from the green before descending gradually. An aiming flag waves from the middle of the fairway there. The deck of the clubhouse provides good views of players coming in.

On the front side, it's generally clear where the ball should go. Not so on the back, which has a number of blind tees and very sharp doglegs. Taken as a whole, the two sides combine to present a sort of golfing trip through the Fun House—around every corner is a surprise.

No. 10 was shortened a bit when the tee box was rebuilt and moved as part of the driving range construction. The range now runs down its right side. The number two handicap, it's a 450-yard par 4. An unrestricted fairway bends a bit to the right at the 150-yard marker. More troublesome than the bend is the grass valley that cuts across the fairway there. And sand surrounds the hole.

A brief walk through the woods leads to the No. 11 tee, which is elevated and looks out onto a fairway dotted at the sides with traps. The terrain falls away on both sides closer to the green. At 410 yards, this par 4 has trouble for anyone not playing in the short grass. There is plenty of sand at the green, too.

The only par 3 on this side is No. 12, just 140 yards long. The green, however, is three times as wide as it is deep—47 yards by 16—and the traps in front of it are fortified with railroad ties between sand and green. It is also particularly difficult to read.

The tee at No. 13, a 375-yard par 4, looks out at an aiming flag providing direction to the hole. The wide fairway rises, crests, and then ambles slightly downhill until the last hundred yards, where it races down to a green surrounded by sand and mounds. The green has long suffered from lack of sunlight, sitting as it does almost at the floor of a valley and surrounded by tall trees. Behind and below the green is the next tee.

No. 14 begins by racing up the first 80 yards. It is a very blind tee shot—almost like shooting over a wall of grass—to a wide fairway that stretches out a couple of hundred yards before falling into a steep, small valley. On the right side of this 490-yard par 5 are deep woods. And when the fairway climbs up from the valley it takes a severe dogleg right; trees fill the elbow. The green can be reached in two great shots, the second a blind shot over tall trees to a smallish green. There is sand at the flat green. From any angle, this is a lot of golf hole.

No. 15, a 315-yard par four, begins straight and bends left when it reaches the valley. In the last hundred yards the fairway drops, then begins rising to the green, in front of which is a sand trap. Overhitting the approach here sends the ball off the side of the green and into deep woods. Even the green is tough because it is sloped forward and, like all the greens at Sleepy Hollow, is fast. Putting right off it is quite possible.

No. 16 has woods all down the left side and the fairway narrows when the rough on the right suddenly drops off. This 360-yard par 4 has a narrow landing area for the drive and a slightly elevated green guarded on the left by a tall old hardwood. There is sand, of course, at the green.

No. 17 is the rare tee here that does not require length, only accuracy. Well, that's not always true. Paul Rowland, a retired librarian from *The Plain Dealer*, for lack of length once hit eight consecutive tee shots into the small lake in front of the tee. Rowland saved himself an ignominious 30 by dropping a long putt, penciling in a 29. He still answers when people ask for the Legend of Sleepy Hollow.

Once over the pretty lake on this 265-yard par 4, the fairway takes a 90-degree left turn. In the elbow of the dogleg are tall trees, so cutting the corner is virtually impossible.

No. 18 is a 400-yard par 4, a straight hole with few difficulties. A couple of trees mark the rough on the sides, and the fairway dips a bit before the green. At the sloped green are sand traps. Like many of the holes at Sleepy Hollow, this one calls for big hitting and fearless putting.

On any ranking of area courses, Sleepy Hollow will rank very high. With the new clubhouse and related amenities, it has been transformed from a very tough course to a glamorous one. It is easy to forget that this course and facility is owned and operated by the government. It sets a standard for all public courses.

Sleepy Hollow Golf Course
9445 Brecksville Rd.
Brecksville, OH 44141   Phone: 526-4285

| Manager: | Jim Chambers |
| Pro: | John Fiander, PGA |

18 holes

Tees	Yds.	Course	Slope
Middle:	6335	69.2	118
Forward:	5815	72.7	122

Season:	Mar 18–Nov 25
Hours:	sunrise–sunset
Greens fees:	$8.50 / $16.00
Special rates:	seniors: $6.50 / $13.00
Carts:	$9.00 / $18.00
Tee times:	taken, not required
Practice facilities:	range, putting green
Clubhouse facilities:	snack bar: food, beer, liquor
Outings:	2 rooms available
League play:	various times
Pro shop:	well stocked
Lessons:	$18.00 per 1/2 hr.; by appointment
Ranger:	daily
New features:	some tee restoration; new clubhouse is completed and open

Springvale Country Club and Ballroom
North Olmsted

Greens fees here used to be two bits. Of course, there were only five holes then. That was in the late twenties, just before The Crash. A few more holes were added to make a complete nine by the end of the thirties, and in 1953 a back nine was added. The thirties still influence the club; it is also home of the Springvale Ballroom, where big bands play four nights a week.

The clubhouse/pro shop is old-fashioned and very comfortable. The dark woodwork is handsome and the card room downstairs is a wonderful throwback to another era. A long bar dominates the room and stuffed fish and game trophies cover the walls. A screened-in porch almost the width of the clubhouse provides a view of the first tee. Outings are popular here, often catered by Tom's Country Place. A special bakery in Avon provides the Danish.

A local rule is often invoked on No. 1, a 323-yard par 4. Just in front of the tee is a lake. Players dribbling their balls into the water have to shoot from the forward tee on the other side of the water hazard. It speeds play. Once over the water, the hole is straight with some fairway sand on the left side and more sand at the green. The greens here are fast.

No. 2 is a 404-yard par 4, a dogleg right. From the tee, the fairway aims a couple of hundred yards towards a tree line, then bends back to the right. In the elbow of the dogleg are sand, mounds, and deep, deep rough. The large fairway markers, discs of different colors in the fairway, aid club selection. No. 3, a 173-yard par 3, starts at a tee box shaded by shagbark hickories. It ends at a large green with no sand.

No. 5, a 334-yard par 4, bends to the right. An Eisenhower tree is in the fairway near the bend, favoring left-to-right players. On this end of the course it is not unusual to halt play, especially in the evening or early morning, to let deer trot across the fairway.

No. 8 is a 281-yard par 4 with sand on the right side reachable from the tee. There is more sand at the green, a narrow target. No. 9 is a snake. This 444-yard par 5 twists left and right, up and down on its way to the green. There, sand and water sit on the right side.

Care must be taken leaving the 9th green and walking back to the clubhouse. The path goes right in front of the 1st tee. Even if the 9th hole produced a high score, there is no sense in making a bad hole worse . . . by getting beaned.

No. 11, a 476-yard par 5, is the signature hole on this course. The fairway is wide and flat to begin with but drops near the 150-yard marker to a crossing valley and creek. Beyond the water, the green is jammed in the side of a hill, sloping forward. An interesting hole, a very different hole. Some players find it an unfair hole because the average player has to hit a drive, a wedge to the edge of the valley, then a 6- or 7-iron over the valley and the water to a green that is very difficult. Big hitters can reach it in two, but missing or failing to hold the green is costly. Keeping the approach shot beneath the flag effectively cuts in half the size of the target. The path continues to rise toward the next tee.

No. 15, the last par 3, is the only short one: 135 yards. No. 16 is a 407-yard par 4 with big water on the left side of the fairway and sand at the green. No. 17, a 509-yard par 5, is straight to a green with sand on both sides.

The finishing hole is a 312-yard par 4. The tee shot has to carry a tree-lined valley. On the other side, the fairway turns sharply left. The hole can be parred with a couple of well-struck irons. In the elbow of the dogleg is valley and water; the prudent player will play in the fairway and resist trying to cut the corner. Hitting and holding the green is important, too, because the rough falls quickly down the side of a hill and into the lake.

Springvale Country Club and Ballroom

Springvale Country Club and Ballroom. What a glorious name for a golf course! While the name is fancier than the amenities here, the course provides a few noteworthy holes and a good challenge to area players. Four nights a week, it also provides big band music for people who appreciate the box step. A most elegant combination.

Springvale Country Club and Ballroom
5873 Canterbury Rd.
North Olmsted, OH 44070   Phone: 777-0678

Owner: Rose Scheeff
General Manager: Bill Scheeff
Assistant Manager: Jan Spisak

18 holes

Tees	Yds.	Course	Slope
Middle:	5911	67.9	110
Back:	6264	68.8	113
Forward:	5290	69.3	110

Season: year-round
Hours: sunrise–sunset
Greens fees: $6.75 / $12.00 wkdays; $7.75 / $16.00 wkends
Special rates: $28.00 for 2 people w/ cart, Mon, Tues & Thu a.m.
Carts: $8.00 / $16.00
Tee times: taken wkends
Practice facilities: range, putting green
Clubhouse facilities: food, beer, liquor; private rooms; lockers & showers; ballroom dancing Wed, Fri, Sat, Sun
Outings: available
League play: Mon–Fri; one mixed league on Sat
Pro shop: lightly stocked
Lessons: not available
Ranger: when necessary
New features: driving range; adding 4th set of tees

Sweetbriar Golf & Pro Shop
Avon Lake

There are 27 holes at Sweetbriar, 9,159 yards over fairly flat terrain for a par of 107. There are also two good practice greens, a driving range, a huge pro shop, and a nice clubhouse.

Recently, a woman playing in a Red Cross outing was waiting, on the 7th tee of the third nine, for the green to clear. No. 7 is a 163-yard par 3. A playing partner suggested she hit without waiting. No chance, he said, of getting the ball to the green. She reached for her trusty 4-wood and hit a nice shot. It bounced onto the green, bounced off the flag, and bounced into the hole. The people putting were surprised. So was she. For her hole-in-one, she received a Lincoln Town Car for one year.

The course is open year-round and has especially nice decorations at Christmas. Lessons are offered and the teaching staff includes two members of the LPGA. Do men or women make the better teacher? Pro Joe Lombardi, PGA, said, "Our women pros have a lot of students and a lot of repeat business, so they must be doing something right." Lombardi's personal record on the front and middle nines is 66.

The clubhouse holds 75 people and the pavilions hold 200 each. It is a popular course for outings as well as leagues, of which more than five dozen play here. Over the course of a year, about 120,000 nine-hole rounds are played.

The first hole is a par 5 of 523 yards. It is straight and runs parallel to a railroad line (o.b.) on the left. It plays tougher than it looks because of two trees crowding the fairway about 250 yards out. The green is big and rolling and not particularly fast. No. 2, a par 4 of 372 yards, continues along the edge

Sweetbriar Golf & Pro Shop

of the course. It is o.b. all the way down the left side; the right side has a smattering of tall trees.

Enough of the warm-up holes. No. 3 is a 449-yard par 4—not beautiful, but tough. Again, o.b. down the left side. The hole starts out to the right and then bends back to the left. It's a wide fairway, but a long way in to the elevated green.

No. 5 has a wide creek flowing across the fairway about 60 yards before the green. Getting to the green on this 324-yard par 4 is not difficult as long as the ball stays in the fairway. This is the last of a series of holes around the perimeter of the course, and has o.b. going down the left side.

No. 6 is a blind tee shot, a par 4 of 386 yards and a dogleg right. There is plenty of room on the left side to land a drive. Drivers with "lazy wrists" or slices will find themselves between trees and mounds, unable to go for the green. A wide creek passes in front of the green.

No. 9 is a par 4 of 417 yards. It is a slight dogleg left; once around the shallow dogleg, it's straight in.

The second nine begins with a 349-yard dogleg left. This par 4 requires a drive to the right side of the fairway for a clear approach. Trees make the hole more narrow at the dogleg. On the left side of the fairway is the driving range (mats only). Many players will break a Rule of Golf here by hitting stray practice balls back to the range. No practice during a match.

No. 12, a 523-yard par 5, is a dogleg right and the inside of the turn is filled with mounds and brush and trees. It takes almost every player three good shots to reach in regulation.

The tee shot on No. 13, a 156-yard par 3, has to clear a sizable lake. No. 14 is a 398-yard par 4. The number two handicap hole, it is pretty straight and has a few trees at the edges. A lake sits in front of the tee and the green has mounds on the sides. No. 15 is a tight, 336-yard par 4 that bends a bit to the right at the 150-yard marker and crosses water before the elevated green.

No. 17, a 522-yard par 5, has some water in front of the tee that is merely decorative. The fairway begins bending to the left after 120 yards or so. From 300 yards in to the green, stands of trees line the rough on both sides. No. 18 is much shorter, a par 5 of only 477 yards. Trees line much of the right side and the driving range lines the left.

Those two nines were built in 1964. The third nine was built in 1981. It is substantially shorter and has only one par 4 longer than 400 yards. Several of the holes are not very distinguished. On the scorecard, the holes are not listed 1 through 9, but 19 through 27. Somehow, it doesn't feel right to refer to a hole as No. 24. And most players look to the clubhouse for the 19th hole. But Sweetbriar runs a good course and a fine clubhouse, so they can call the holes whatever they like.

No. 19 is a 249-yard par 4 with trees on both sides of the fairway and a good-sized moat before the green. But getting on the putting surface is easily accomplished with a couple of irons. No. 20 is a 157-yard par 3 over a lake and offers a big target. The greens on this nine are generally sloped. Short game here is vital.

No. 25, a par 3 of 173 yards, is tougher than its measurements. Plenty of tall trees lean in on both sides, protecting a small green. No. 26, the number one handicap on this nine, is a 401-yard par 4 that bends to the right. A creek flows across the fairway close to the green, which slopes forward.

The final hole is another par 4, this one 309 yards also crossed by a creek before the green. The creek continues up the left side to the green, which is tucked into a stand of trees to the right. Not an easy target.

Management here understands that golf is not a seasonal malady but an addiction that must be sated year-round. If the snow is not deep, there is play here. And then the clubhouse provides all the coffee needed to warm up—on the house.

Sweetbriar Golf & Pro Shop

Sweetbriar Golf & Pro Shop
750 Jaycox Rd.
Avon Lake, OH 44012   Phone: 871-0822; 933-9001

Pro / Manager: Joe Lombardi, PGA

27 holes

Courses 1&2				Courses 1&3		
Tees	Yds.	Course	Slope	Yds.	Course	Slope
Middle:	6311	68.5	106	5895	66.2	100
Back:	6491	68.7	106	6075	66.3	100
Forward:	5612	72.1	112	5505	69.5	108

Courses 2&3			
Tees	Yds.	Course	Slope
Middle:	6112	67.4	104
Back:	6292	67.5	104
Forward:	5411	71.1	110

Season:	year-round
Hours:	sunrise–sunset
Greens fees:	$7.00 / $16.00 wkdays; $8.50 / $16.00 wkends
Special rates:	$17.50 per person for 18 holes & 1/2 cart, wkdays
Carts:	$8.25 / $16.50
Tee times:	not taken
Practice facilities:	range
Clubhouse facilities:	snack bar: food, beer
Outings:	catering available
League play:	daily
Pro shop:	well stocked
Lessons:	$25.00 per 1/2 hr.; by appointment; 4 pros on staff
Ranger:	yes
Special rules:	no alcoholic beverages allowed on property

Tam O'Shanter Public Golf Course
Canton

Though Canton is outside an "easy drive" of downtown, there are two good reasons to make the trip: the Hills Course and the Dales course. Doubtless Canton has other virtues, but Tam O'Shanter, where Hills and Dales are found, is reason enough. Tam O'Shanter is singular in many respects, including its promotion of the game. It is the only course to take a billboard ad so drivers on I-77 are reminded of the Stark County course. Owner Chuck Bennell regularly brings groups from out of state to play his and other nearby courses as well as visit the pro football Hall of Fame.

When Bennell was told not to bother promoting his courses or the area because it was not the Carolinas or Florida, he refused to listen. Michiganders, Pennsylvanians, and Ohioans play at Tam O'Shanter because Bennell provides them with a country club atmosphere, two distinctly different courses reflecting classic golf course architecture, and a clubhouse that should be surrounded by magnolias. It is an old-fashioned, three-story house with a half-dozen tall columns supporting the broad porch roof.

The courses were built as part of a housing development, the Hills and Dales project, which is just across the street. Had the project been successful, and a building boom continued, backyards and basements would today be where a driving range and practice green are. Development was slowed first by the Depression, then by World War II.

"The Dales course opened in 1928," Bennell said, "and the Hills course opened in 1931. When Hills opened, Mr. Harris added some hoopla because of the Depression. He brought Walter Hagen and Gene Sarazen in from the Western Open to play the dedication round. And a Massillon bootlegger made sure the refreshments were spirited."

Bennell pointed out the style of golf architecture that marks his 60-year-old layouts. "They say the old-time architects didn't design courses so much as they found them." The Dales Course was designed by Leonard Maycomber, the construction superintendent for Donald Ross when Ross created Canton Brookside in the early twenties. The Hills Course was designed by Merle Paul.

The clubhouse is suitable for a formal dinner; the pro shop is first rate. Counting clubhouse, courses, and history, Tam O'Shanter would have to be considered one of the top public courses in northern Ohio.

The Dales Course plays 6,248 yards, par 70. No. 1 is a 377-yard dogleg left and the whole fairway slopes that way as well. A big, soft draw will have the envy of waiting players. In the elbow of the dog, white stakes mark o.b. to protect players on an adjacent hole. Lesser hitters will have just as good a chance at par by playing in the fairway. There are more trees lining the right side of the hole and plenty of sand at the green.

No. 4 is a straight 411-yard par 4. The last few hundred yards of fairway are lined on both sides with pine trees. The old hardwoods to the right of the green should not be a hazard, but protect the next tee. To the right of the green is a new wooden staircase built of wood pieces the size of railroad ties. It leads to the No. 5 tee.

There, the drive is a blind shot. This 348-yard par 4 can delight as well as confound. The fairway does more than rise—it has a steep hill in the middle of it. Hitting over the hill is not difficult and provides an easy shot to the green, but missing a tee shot can be costly. This is one of many holes that plays better with practice.

No. 8 is only a 386-yard par 4, but because it can call for a variety of shots and is a tight hole, it's the number one handicap. The fairway is quite hilly and takes a dogleg right getting to a green with mounds on both sides.

The back side starts off with a very challenging par 4; No. 10 is 439 yards bending to the right almost off the tee. Players grateful for the opportunity to use their slices learn quickly that accuracy does not lose its value here. It is a narrow, hilly fairway and landing area. There is fairway sand to the right front of the green and more sand on the right side of the green. The green is elevated and calls for a most difficult approach: a high, long iron.

No. 14 aims downhill 167 yards to a par 3 green that rests in front of the equipment shed. There is sand behind the green to slow balls otherwise headed for the broad side of the barn. It's a short walk around the barn to the tee box of one of the most interesting holes at Tam O'Shanter.

No. 15, a 405-yard par 4, tumbles down into a valley, turns right and climbs the side of a hill. There is a light bulb to the right of the tee; when it lights, it signals that it is safe to hit. The switch is turned by players in the valley. This is a blind tee shot with o.b. on the left. The green has sand on the right side. This is certainly one of the holes that the course architect "found."

No. 16 doesn't have the excitement of the previous hole, but this 358-yard par 4 has a blind approach shot. A straight hole, there is fairway sand on the right side near the 150-yard marker. The green, however, sits in a small valley. A power line stands behind it and can be used as an aiming point.

The finishing hole is a straightaway par 4 of 408 yards beginning from an elevated tee and finishing at a green with sand on the right side.

After Dales, real golfers relax over lunch and maybe a brief nap before heading out to the first tee on the Hills Course. It is more open than Dales and shorter, too. No. 1 is a 381-yard par 4 that plays straight, though not level. Even in the heart of the fairway, un-level lies are to be expected. Near the green is sand on the right front; getting out of it is a matter of lofting the ball eight feet high.

No. 2 is a 386-yard par 4 from a blind tee. The narrow fairway rises toward a dogleg right; terrain on both sides rises. There is sand on the right front of the green—so much that the area of sand is probably greater than that of the green. While these greens are not going to hit two digits on the Stimpmeter, neither are they slow.

No. 5 is only 434 yards, a very short par 5. But the fairway narrows on this dogleg right and there are o.b. stakes all the way down the right side. In the last 150 yards the rough on both sides rises, giving the hole a riverbed look. Tall trees close in as golfers near the green and hardwoods form a backdrop for the approach.

The back side in begins with a 369-yard par 4. It has a wide fairway, some pretty hardwoods on the sides, and rolling terrain. Near the small green, the fairway narrows and a grass bunker appears up on the right side.

No. 12 is a short par 3, but anyone coming up short on the 133-yard hole will have to play out of a sand trap 30 feet across and as wide as the fairway. No. 13 calls for a big and accurate drive. This 409-yard par 4 is straight enough, but the green is elevated as well as protected by sand. Players overhitting the green will search for balls at the bottom of a hill.

No. 15, a 421-yard par 4, is another long and straight golf hole. The tee provides one of the prettiest views on the course, looking out at the fairway, an adjacent fairway, the clubhouse in the distance, and along that same line, a stand of hardwoods on a hill. Fifty yards from the green is a grass bunker and at the green are two sand traps.

No. 16 is the last par 5 of the day. Its fairway rises and falls like a children's roller coaster: delightful, but not scary. There is fairway sand close to the green and more sand on the left front and left side of the green. It takes three solid shots to get in position to birdie here.

No. 17 is a long par 3 of 184 yards, but slightly downhill. Missing the target here can leave the ball in a front trap (which has an island of rough in the middle), a rear trap, or hiding behind one of the trees backing the green. The finishing hole is a comfortable, 267-yard par 4 that says, "if you haven't won the match yet, don't plan to win it here."

It's a bit of a drive to Canton and the two courses at Tam O'Shanter, but the only regret of most players who make the trip is not playing both courses the same day.

Tam O'Shanter Public Golf Course
5055 Hills & Dales Rd. NW
Canton, OH 44708   Phone: 477-5111; 800-462-9964

President: Charles Bennell
Pro: Martin Roesink

36 holes	Hills Course			Dales Course		
Tees	Yds.	Course	Slope	Yds.	Course	Slope
Middle:	6054	67.6	103	6249	68.9	107
Back:	6385	69.1	104	6569	70.4	110
Forward:	5076	67.4	102	5384	69.7	109

Season:	Mar–Dec
Hours:	sunrise–sunset
Greens fees:	$9.00 / $18.00
Special rates:	season pass available; special rates available
Carts:	$8.00 / $16.00
Tee times:	taken wkdays; required wkends, holidays
Practice facilities:	range, putting green, chipping green
Clubhouse facilities:	food, beer, liquor
Outings:	available
League play:	various times
Pro shop:	well stocked
Lessons:	available
Ranger:	certain days only

Thunder Hill Golf Club
Madison

The patron saint here must be Minihaha. A few years ago, gamefish swam across the fairways. One green appears designed by earthquake. Course literature proudly describes it as "the world's greatest challenge in golf."

Welcome to Thunder Hill, the public course of mythical proportions.

With more than 70 lakes and ponds on the course, some players count "balls lost" along with strokes played. Others simply refuse to make the trip to Thunder Hill, citing tales told by friends of friends, stories that make a round of golf sound as difficult as an infantry charge.

It's only a golf course.

Still, it is unlike any other course in the area and its reputation for severely challenging players is well deserved. Joe Raisian and Mike Mondy run the course. Neither is shy about singing its praises. "If you hit it sideways, you're going to lose 50 balls out here," Mondy said. "The course weeds out hackers—they're not going to come back."

When Mondy and Raisian started managing the course, their first concern was preventing it from being grown over. They took a lease on it in July 1989. "When we came out, the greens were diseased. We aerated the third week of August, that's how bad it was. They looked like this table," he said, knocking his knuckles on a rough tabletop in the clubhouse. "And they were rock hard."

The rest of the course was not any better. "We couldn't even find the lakes," Raisian said about the overgrown rough.

The land was an apple orchard before Fred Slagle, real estate agent, created a country club in 1975. Drainage can be a problem on the hilly course. In 1990, the Summer of Wet, the ponds overflowed and sent aquatic life sliding across fairways. The ponds are filled with all sorts of fish: bass, bluegill, perch, walleye, and an Asian import, the amur. The amur thrives on algae and is used to clear ponds. Don't bother tossing the Zebco in the trunk next to the sticks, though; fishing (except for balls) is not allowed. The managers sell the stock to a fish broker who regularly visits the course.

Four sets of tees mean the course can play as long as 7,323 yards or as short as 5,638. In addition to 76 ponds (who's counting?), the course is further tightened by 80 sand traps and plenty of trees.

The cart paths here often call for four-wheel drive. The carts, incidentally, are equipped with sand rakes. They'll double as ball retrievers for the unwary who show up without one.

Tough as the course is, Thunder Hill is a fine place for an outing, especially when the scramble format is used, allowing every member of a team to contribute and balls sent to sleep with the fishes to be forgotten. And every serious golfer should play Thunder Hill at least once, just as everyone should jump from an airplane. For some, once will be enough. For others, there will never be enough.

The first hole looks out over a couple of ponds and runs straight until it meets a pine grove. The fairway then veers right. There are plenty of trees on the course, but very little underbrush. The rough is minimal, and chipping out from the woods is usually a simple matter. The last 150 yards of No. 1 are lined with hardwoods on the right and pines on the left. The green is surrounded by four sand traps.

There is a lake edged with willows and cattails in front of the No. 2 tee. This first par 5 is an easy 462 yards and reachable in two. A serious slice off the tee will put the ball over some mounds that separate the fairway from the practice range. The difficulty then is not finding a ball; there are hundreds there. Its finding the one you just hit.

There are many handsome tees on this course and No. 3, the first par 3, is one of them. It is a short hole, only 137 yards.

Thunder Hill Golf Club

The cart path runs between two ponds in front of the tee. A generous green is backed up by a beautiful stand of pines. Some sand is found on the right side of the green.

No. 4 is a long par 4, 428 yards. Ten traps narrow the fairway and water waits to catch wild slices or hooks off the tee. No. 5, a par 4 of 385 yards, is very tight off the tee but the landing area opens considerably. The right and front of the green is protected by water; the left and rear have traps.

No. 7 is a 423-yard par 4 and a big 50-degree dogleg. Water fills much of the right side and shows up again near the green. Down the left side of the fairway stands a straight line of pines. Sand traps wait at the green.

No. 8, a 551-yard par 5, calls for two shots totaling 480 yards or an odd lay-up. There is enough water on this hole to launch a small fleet, and some of it sits in the fairway. The fairway itself is narrow and the green is well bunkered.

At No. 9, the tee points toward civilization—the clubhouse. Getting there, however, calls for a long iron or fairway wood. This par 3 measures 192 yards over substantial water. The view from the tee, over the water to the three-story clubhouse, warrants a postcard. The green here is generous and trapped.

A quick stop at the clubhouse and players can emerge with a six-pack of beer and a Thunder Dog. It may be that the front side, played from the middle tees, proves to be less than mythical. Careful players might wonder why the course has the reputation it has. Challenging, to be sure, but not lethal.

Get ready.

No. 10 is a 381-yard par 4 that calls for a blind tee shot to land in a narrow fairway. Water lurks nearby. It is a dogleg right and the green, with water right and rear, is beautifully framed with trees.

No. 12, a 497-yard par 5, lets players stumble directly into harm's way. The fairway on this hole is filled with ambushes: one big tree, four ponds, four sand traps. Woods close in around the edges. It calls for remarkable accuracy and sound shot planning. And luck.

And No. 13 suggests strongly that there is brutal golf ahead. A narrow fairway, as it nears the 150-yard marker, suddenly drops down and sharply to the right, then zooms up again to the green. An even 400 yards long, a good drive in the narrow fairway will leave a mid-iron to the green. A super drive will leave the super driver in a super ditch. About seven ponds can come into play on this hole. Thick groves of trees here are omnivorous, swallowing hooks and slices alike.

At No. 14, a 377-yard par 4, vestiges of the orchard remain and the rich smell of apples fills the summer air. This is no tee for a lapse in concentration. There is a valley in front of the tee beyond which the fairway is closely guarded on both sides by trees. The opening for the drive is only about 35 yards wide. Just a slight draw will send the ball into a pine grove. Three large ponds are draped in a line across the rough and fairway near the green.

No. 15 is another par 4, only 362 yards from the regulation tees. The fairway starts straight, narrows dramatically, then descends to a sizable green. Surprise—there is water in front of the green. As on many holes here, it is wise to look twice before swinging. A glance at the scorecard here will point to a disturbing conclusion: this nine is getting harder. The back side is far more narrow and has more hills, water, and sand.

From one of the higher points on the course, the 16th tee looks down on a short par 5, only 453 yards. But hardwoods line both sides of the narrow fairway and rarely bounce mishits back, so accuracy is again vital. There is a slight dogleg right about 100 yards from the green. Plenty of sand, too, on both sides of this fairway. The long and narrow green has a huge hump near the rear. It's not likely the flag would be placed behind it (one would hope not, anyway). But putting from back there will be unimaginably difficult. Next to the green is a beautiful beech tree. Its bark is filled with what appear to be scars in the shape of putter heads.

This is clearly not a course for beginners or hackers. But for a player who shoots in the 80s, it will add another dimension to the game. Bring a snorkle.

Thunder Hill Golf Club

Thunder Hill Golf Club
7050 Griswold Rd.
South Madison, OH 44057   Phone: 298-3474

Superintendent: Michael Mondy
Director of Golf: Joseph Raisian

18 holes

Tees	Yds.	Course	Slope
Middle:	6859	73.6	131
Back:	7323	76.1	151
Way Back:	7323	78.0	n/r
Forward:	5638	71.5	127

Season: Mar 1–Nov 30
Hours: 7:00 a.m.–8:00 p.m.
Greens fees: 18 holes & 1/2 cart: $22.00 wkdays; $27.00 wkends
                        Mon special: $15.00 for 18 holes & 1/2 cart
                        evening specials; memberships available
Carts: $9.00 / $15.00
Tee times: required wkends
Practice facilities: short-iron range, putting green
Clubhouse facilities: snack bar & lounge: food, beer, liquor; banquet facilities
Outings: regular events; private outings available
League play: traveling leagues
Pro shop: lightly stocked
Lessons: not available
Ranger: wkends and for large outings
Special rules: carts mandatory Sat & Sun 6 a.m.–2 p.m.
New features: cart paths being added, woods & brush cleared between holes; mounds around No. 13 green

Valleaire Golf Club
Hinckley

Golf courses are built for all sorts of reasons: as a family business, for a land bank, to fill a market niche. Here, the course was built because the Knights of Columbus were having difficulty securing tee times for their traveling league. Members purchased property in the north of Medina County and built a gorgeous little course.

Valleaire is very playable, a course where average golfers will find themselves looking at a few birdie putts. It also has some difficult holes and tough greens, however, and staring at a putt for triple bogey will not be a rarity. It's a beautiful layout, cut from softly hilly forest and manicured with a professional touch.

It begins with a short par 4, only 273 yards of straight fairway to a big, round green with a tall stand of pines behind it. It's not really representative of the holes to follow, such as No. 2. At the tee of this 447-yard par 4, civilization is suddenly left behind. Getting on this green in regulation is very difficult, for reasons of distance alone. The fairway narrows as it heads toward an elevated green, one of the trademarks of this course. The 150-yard markers are the best in the area: wooden planks hanging from pipes in the rough. In addition to being elevated, this long and narrow green also has the stand of pines behind it.

No. 3 is another long one, a par 5 of 520 yards. Getting on in three strokes should not be a problem for most players because the fairway is generous and the big green has no sand protecting it. On the right side of the fairway, however, past the very rough rough, is o.b. The left side is a bit more forgiving, with just a few trees to get in the way.

Valleaire Golf Club

No. 4 is an uphill par 4 of 336 yards. One hundred thirty yards from the tee is the Valleaire version of the Eisenhower tree standing in the fairway. Off to the right is more o.b., and the approach shot follows a fairway that bends to the right, so the tee shot is an important shot on this hole. Again, it's a big green, cared for (as are all the greens here, it is obvious) with gentle hands.

The first par 3 shows up at No. 7 and is a 184 yarder calling for an iron of some length and accuracy. Here, as at a number of other tee boxes, flower boxes spilling over with colorful blooms add to the beauty of the layout.

No. 8, the second par 5 on this side, is a straight 475-yard hole with a fairway that is both rolling and narrow. On the right side, the terrain rises and is covered with thick underbrush. The trademark elevated green is large on this hole.

No. 9 is a par 3 of 148 yards, much of it over water. Shade is provided at the tee by an old and stately oak tree, and the lake separating the tee from the green has a fountain. Some Canada geese regularly lounge about, close to water's edge and unaffected by the spouting from the fountain or the occasional curses from the tee.

The back side begins with a par 4 of 417 yards parallel to the first hole. Its narrow fairway is cut through by a creek at about a 150 yards from the tee. The green is elevated but has no sand.

No. 11 is a 325-yard par 4, a straight hole with water in front of the green. Old hardwoods stand on both sides of the fairway, not so thick as to prevent finding a ball, but thick enough that the recovery shot can be little more than a chip back to the fairway.

No. 13 is (yet another) straight par 4, this one 320 yards. With a mere two decent strokes, a birdie appears on the horizon.

No. 18, a 402-yard par 4, has a creek running across the fairway when the weather and precipitation is normal here. Long hitters can reach it on their way to the green.

Water is much more important on the back side than on the front. The course takes advantage of the land, the beautiful and old hardwood forests, and offers players a slightly hilly round of golf. The greens, most of them elevated, are kept in great shape, and few have sand near or around them. The old, two-story frame clubhouse is as comfortable as an old K of C hall.

Valleaire Golf Club
6969 Boston Rd.
Hinckley, OH 44233   Phone: 237-9191

Manager: Pat Arnold

18 holes

Tees	Yds.	Course	Slope
Middle:	6067	68.4	113
Back:	6442	70.2	117
Forward:	5552	70.9	116

Season: Apr–Nov
Hours: sunrise–sunset
Greens fees: $7.50 / $10.75 wkdays; $8.75 / $15.75 wkends
Special rates: seniors: $5.25 / $7.50
Carts: $9.00 / $17.00
Tee times: required wkends
Practice facilities: putting green
Clubhouse facilities: food, beer, liquor
Outings: available
League play: various times
Pro shop: lightly stocked
Lessons: not available
Ranger: daily

Western Reserve Golf & Country Club
Sharon Center

This is club manager Bernie Steward's ninth year in Ohio. He came from Nebraska at the urging of a friend. "Weather's a little better here," he said. He runs, for owner Doug Ducker, this 25-year-old course that used to be a farm. Plenty of league play fills the tees from Monday through Friday. Between a growing junior program, the league play, and regular play, Steward no longer markets the course for outings.

The clubhouse sits above the practice green and looks down on the course before it. It's a building with an equally wide porch in front. The course and the clubhouse have an old-fashioned informality about them that is fun. Clearly, the mortgage doesn't rest on a game of golf here. Golf is played here for the pleasure of it.

Western Reserve is a short and tight layout with a couple of holes that make little sense, but who's to criticize.

Play opens on the number one handicap hole. No. 1 is a 394-yard par 4 and big dogleg right. Neither short nor tight, this hole makes plenty of sense. In the elbow of the dogleg a stream meanders between the 1st and 10th fairways. Over on the left side of the bend there is deep rough and a small pond. About 180 yards from the green there are two fairway traps on the left side. A nicely trimmed apron leads up to a large green. A tough opening hole.

No. 2 is a 361-yard par 4, lined on both sides with trees and offering a difficult landing area for tee shots. A reasonably straight fairway leads to another large green. But on the right side of this green is a lake easily found by players unable to control their slices.

No. 4, a 378-yard par 4, is lined with trees all along the right side; there are just a few trees on the left. From about 200 yards to 140 yards from the green, a C-shaped pond hides beyond the left rough.

At 415 yards, No. 5 is one of the shortest par 5s around. It is a straight hole with water near the green. Just before the apron, a small pond cuts into the fairway. There are some mounds at the green but no sand here. A real birdie opportunity. It's followed by another par 5, this one more reasonable in length. No. 6 is 479 yards. And it's a driving hole—plenty of room.

No. 8, a 352-yard par 4 is straight a hundred yards before it bends sharply left. In the corner are trees, deep rough, and o.b. It's a hole of questionable design. The right side—the edge of the course—is o.b. as well. Pines and an occasional oak tree line the hole on the left side, and the green, with a large sand trap on the front left, is slightly elevated.

No. 9 is a difficult hole for club selection. This third par 3 on the front is only 162 yards, but all of them steeply uphill. It is virtually a blind tee shot. In front of the tee is a small pond and over to the right is a trash dump. Missing the green short and left can send the ball into a valley filled with trees and thick underbrush.

No. 10 begins in front of the clubhouse at a pretty, elevated tee. The par 4, 355-yard hole is straight with hardwoods lining both sides. There is a creek along the left edge that winds its way into the fairway close to the green. The last 150 yards of fairway roll up and down—mostly down—to the green.

No. 11 is only 262 yards, but many of those yards are lake. The landing area for the drive on this par 4 is minimal. A creek begins at the tee on the left side and runs out 50 yards before cutting across the fairway. Then it flows up the right side into a substantial lake. The lake comes across the right front of the green. Behind the green are 25 yards of rough and then another, larger lake. The left side of the fairway is lined with pines and the green is slightly elevated. It's a tough hole, one that calls for some accurate iron shots.

No. 13 is a short par 5. At 434 yards, par seems to be an easy target. In the mid-1980s, the East Ohio Gas Company held an outing here. On this hole, Don Franceski hit his usual big and straight drive, then nailed a 5-wood. Double eagle. Franceski avoided a lot of trouble with his second shot. The hole bends to the right near the green and, on the left side, a lake waits for balls. Hidden in the right rough, about 80 yards from the green, is a small pond.

No. 14, a 345-yard par 4, is the number two handicap hole. It's a big dogleg right and rises ever so slightly. In the elbow on the right side is a small lake. Across the fairway there is a sand trap. The left side is o.b., private property marked with a split rail fence. The green is elevated and pines stand behind it.

No. 16, a straight 357-yard par 4, has a few trees on either side but a generous fairway. Close to the green there is water on the right side, but it should not come into play. The approach shot is made more difficult by a stand of hardwoods guarding the left side of the green.

The finishing hole is another short one, a par 4 of only 234 yards. It's far from the prettiest hole on the course. A pond sits in front of the green here. After holing out, it's an uphill walk to the clubhouse and its wide porch and fine views.

Like many area courses, Western Reserve was transformed from farmland to fairway. It is reached via a couple of two-land blacktops and rarely promotes itself. A good little hideaway for the salesperson who keeps sticks in the trunk. While not especially notable, neither is it pretentious. And it has one of the best front porches in the area.

Western Reserve Golf & Country Club
1543 Fixler Rd.
Sharon Center, OH 44274   Phone: 239-9902; 239-2839

Manager: Bernie Steward

Tees	Yds.	Course	Slope
Middle:	5545	69.1	108
Back:	5923	71.4	104
Forward:	4516	71.2	101

Season: year-round
Hours: 6:00 a.m.–10:00 p.m. in summer
Greens fees: $8.00 / $13.00 wkdays; $9.00 / $17.00 wkends
Special rates: seniors: $28.50 for 18 holes, 2 people & cart,
                       wkdays before noon
                       couples rate: $15.00 / $20.00
                       wkday early bird rates: $6.00 / $10.00
Carts: $9.00 / $17.00
Tee times: taken wkends and holidays
Practice facilities: driving range, putting green
Clubhouse facilities: snack bar: beer & wine
Outings: available
League play: wknights and three weekday mornings
Pro shop: lightly stocked
Lessons: $15.00 / 45 minutes, by appointment
Ranger: wkends

Willow Creek Golf Club
Vermilion

Frank Cisterino, PGA, has been the owner here only a handful of years. Under previous ownership, upkeep was less than thorough and Cisterino has spent long work weeks bringing the course back to its original condition. It is almost an antique; the first nine were carved out of the woods at the end of World War II. Twenty years later, a second nine was created.

Century oaks provide dramatic and beautiful scenery, whether budding in spring, providing deep shade in the summer, or lining the forest floor with golden leaves in autumn. In addition to the oaks and willows there are a half-dozen apple trees. In the late summer and fall, they produce a sweet and crisp fruit, favored by a few golfers as well as families of deer that live around the course.

Cisterino does not know the course record because the course, until late last year, had not been rated by the USGA. He said several players have turned in scorecards with 64s circled, but the pro won't make anything official until a score is posted in 1992.

The length of the course may change a bit, as well, when it gets measured this season with lasers. Laser or no, it is not a short course. It plays 6,419 yards, par 72. For players using the red tees, it is still a lengthy course: 6,220 yards, par 72. Those figures are according to the scorecard. On numerous holes, the yardage announced at the tee is much shorter. For example, the ninth hole is listed as 440 yards on the scorecard, but at the tee the sign reads 371. The scorecard has No. 10 and No. 14 at 430 and 450 yards, though the signs at the tee boxes say 403 and 406, respectively.

In addition to bringing course conditions back up to standard, Cisterino continues a program of adding sand traps.

Eighteen leagues call Willow Creek home, and the course offers a pavilion for outings. It has both driving range and practice green. The pro shop is moderately well stocked and the snack bar offers all that players need. Tee times are taken for league play, and Cisterino is available for players needing lessons.

Starting with the first hole, it is a beautiful course to walk. No. 1 is a long par 4, 396 yards with a leftward bend. It plays into a setting sun in the early evening. But most of the course is laid out north-and-south, adding a distinct measure of comfort to the round. The green is small at the first hole and there is no sand (yet). Like most of the greens here, it is lush and of average speed. Getting down in two should be routine.

No. 2 is a 375-yard par 4, a dogleg left. Forest lines the left side but the fairway is generous. No. 3 is a par 4 of only 277 yards, though given adequate rainfall the second shot must carry water. It's a narrow hole with especially thick woods on the left.

No. 5 is the first of two consecutive par 5s. This tree-lined, 506-yard hole bends softly to the right at first, more seriously so in the final hundred yards. No. 6, an S-shaped par 5 of 475 yards, finishes with an approach over a creek to a green guarded by a century oak.

In the design of these holes, almost a half century ago, distance was important, but not more important than accuracy. No. 8 is a 317-yard par 4 that gives pause to players on the tee. A couple of trees take up almost a third of the fairway only a hundred yards out. Getting around them to the green in regulation can be a simple matter of two well-struck irons.

No. 9 is the signature hole here, but not for its length or difficulty, though a par 4 of 440 yards is no piece of cake. It's a dogleg left crossed diagonally in front of the tee by a creek, which continues up the left side near the green. An old willow squats next to it there. Players don't get to see the green until the second shot.

Willow Creek Golf Club

No. 10 is 430-yard par 4, plenty roomy, though it bends a bit to the right. Trees are not hazardous here, though a few are to be found in the rough on both sides. Trees also form a guard unit behind the green. No. 11 is a virtual hallway of hardwoods leading to the green. It is a 135-yard par 3.

No. 12 is a very tough par 4 of 315 yards. About halfway, the hole turns right. That can't be seen from the tee. A maple sits almost in the middle of the fairway and forces tough choices on the tee. Most players leave the driver in the bag and opt for a more controlled shot.

No. 13, a 530-yard par 5, calls for a draw over the lake in front of the tee and up the fairway, which bends left. It is a generous fairway, though fringed with hardwoods, and it rises toward the green.

No. 14 is another dogleg left. A 450-yard par 4, thick woods on the right side help to narrow the fairway. Near the 150-yard marker, it grows narrower still where trees lean in on each side. From the bend, ground falls to a small green.

Reaching the green at No. 16 calls for three long straight shots. This par 5, which runs along State Route 2, is a straight 595 yards, with only a maple sticking out into the fairway at about 130 yards from the green.

No. 18 is a par 4 of 413 yards (though at the tee, the engraved wooden sign reads 374). A straight hole, woods continue down its left side. On the right are more apple trees—they produce quite a crop. A creek cuts across the fairway in front of the green, which is slightly elevated, and a willow rests on the left side.

Willow Creek is an attractive old course in good hands. It will likely provide great golf for another half century.

Willow Creek Golf Club
15905 Darrow Rd.
Vermilion, OH 44089   Phone: 967-4101

Owner / Pro: Frank Cisterino, PGA

18 holes
Tees   Yds.   Course   Slope
Middle: 6419   n/a   n/a
Forward: 6220   n/a   n/a

Season: Mar–Dec
Hours: sunrise–sunset
Greens fees: $6.50 / $12.00
Special rates: seniors: $3.75 / $7.00 wkdays
                        wkday special: 2 players w/cart $15.00 each;
                        seniors $13.50 each
Carts: $8.00 / $16.00
Tee times: required wkends
Practice facilities: range, putting green
Clubhouse facilities: food, beer
Outings: available; pavilion
League play: wkday mornings & afternoons
Pro shop: lightly stocked
Lessons: $25.00 / 1/2 hr.; by appointment
Ranger: at peak times
New features: adding sand traps

Windmill Lakes Golf Club
Ravenna

This home course of the Kent State University golf team, opened in 1970, was designed by Maryland golf architect Edward Ault, Sr. Herb Page, pro at Windmill Lakes, describes the style of the layout as "typical of that period, with big, rolling greens. Ours average 7,000-8,000 square feet. Three sets of men's tees, big tee boxes. Fifty-four greenside bunkers. And whether you like it or not, it's a big maintenance style."

Getting Mr. Page to talk about his course is a simple matter. Waiting for him to finish can be interminable. "I'm very biased," he said, "but this is one of the top public golf facilities." Biased or not, he is correct.

From the tournament tees (Windmill Lakes hosts qualifying matches for the USGA Public Links Championship), it plays 6,936, par 70.

That is a lot of golf course. The course record is held by Hogan Tour pro Karl Zoller, who helps Page coach at KSU. A few years ago, he fired a 63. The average score posted there is close to 90, Page said. "That's strictly a guess," he said, adding that the typical player at Windmill is an above-average golfer. That could be. Ravenna is off the beaten path and many players consider the trip to be more than a round at the closest public course. It is one well worth planning.

The first hole is a 398-yard par 4 (from the tournament tees it measures 450 yards). The slight dogleg right slopes down from the tee and then bends right. Near the 150-yard marker on the left is a small lake. Oak trees fill the right side of the fairway and traps mark the green.

The green on No. 1 is indicative of the rest: fast, true, and undulating. And the fairway on No. 1 has features that will become come familiar as the round goes on. The turf is thick and healthy, cut to about 1/2 ". It is beautifully manicured and the difference between fairway and rough is substantial. The rough is not of U.S. Open length, but it is rough. The value of staying in the fairway is at a premium here. Such grooming also adds to the physical beauty of the game and can best be appreciated with a view from the tee.

No. 3 is a 361-yard dogleg left best played down the right side for an angle to the green. There is sand on both sides of the fairway and at the green.

No. 4 is a long, 521-yard par 5, the only par 5 on this side. Its length should not be a problem for players who can hit straight. The fairway rises and is narrow. Near the green on the right side is a creek that should not come into play. Closer to the green is a pair of sand bunkers.

No. 5 is a 387-yard par 4 that begins at a slightly elevated tee. Tall hardwoods stretch out 50 yards on either side. Then the fairway opens up. There is water to the right of the fairway and green, and two sand traps at the green.

No. 6 is another reminder to stay straight. A narrow, 397-yard par 4, it goes slightly uphill. A few trees dot either side of the rough until the last 125 yards, where hardwoods become more numerous. At the green, again, more sand traps on either side.

No. 7, a 346-yard par 4, is also straight and narrow. Water shows up on the right side in the landing area and close to the green, where two traps prevent bad hits from caroming into thick woods. The entire left side is o.b.

No. 8 is a beautiful par 3. A big pond lies in front of the green, the largest on the front side. Behind the green is dense underbrush. Along the right side of the hole, tall trees can be troublesome.

The experienced player, reflecting on the difficult greens of the front side, will likely opt for simply chipping the ball directly into each cup on the back side, dispensing with even trying to read them. That only slows play.

No. 10 is another beautiful tee. It looks out on a 387-yard par 4 lined with tall hardwoods that thin out when the fairway bends to the right for the last 140 yards.

No. 11 is a 369-yard par four, again a hole that rewards the accurate shooter. It's straight, but in front and to the left of the green is water. Three sand traps also surround this green.

No. 13 is a 329-yard par 4 that turns left, then right as it makes its way to the green. On the right side, 110 yards from the green, is a sizable pond that cuts into the fairway and makes an already narrow fairway more so. A long, straight drive will frequently find this hidden pond.

The only par 5 on this side is No. 16, a 495-yard hole with a fairway that rises ever so slightly and bends as slightly to the right. From the tee, an average player hitting a good shot will clear the soft turn and save a few yards. A particularly troublesome sand trap yawns right in front of this green.

Many of the tees at Windmill Lakes have flower boxes; No. 17 is one. Besides gorgeous flowers is a sign: "Any person seen to be hitting golf balls at the tower will be lawfully prosecuted to the fullest extent of the law." The warning refers to a tower, off the course to the left, that is about three stories high and resembles a water tower. It is pock-marked by hundreds of dents from outlaw golf balls. Likely the sign and its stern warning incite this attractive crime. The hole plays 390 yards and this par 4 is straightaway. Water lines the left side about 200 yards out, and a small pond is on the right side at about 150 yards from the green, which has sand front and back.

No. 18 is a 380-yard par 4 that slowly rises to a sharply elevated green. With sand traps at right front and left rear encouraging concentration on the approach, it's not an easy finishing hole.

There are amenities here not found at other clubs and the best known is Cipriano's, a restaurant and lounge frequented by area residents as well as players.

Herb Page also runs one of the best pro shops in northeast Ohio. The PGA once named him "Merchandiser of the

Year." Tee times are not so important during the week but very important on weekends and holidays, when the course offers a credit-card guarantee.

Windmill Lakes Golf Club
6544 Rte. 14
Ravenna, OH 44266   Phone: 297-0440

Director of Golf: Herb Page

18 holes

Tees	Yds.	Course	Slope
Middle:	6132	71.7	123
Back:	6503	73.4	128
Forward:	5368	72.7	120

Season: late Mar–late Oct (pro shop open all year)
Hours: 7:00 a.m.–9:00 p.m.
Greens fees: $9.00 / $18.00 wkdays; $12.00 / $24.00 wkends
Special rates: seniors: $17.00 for 18 holes & 1/2 cart, Mon, Tue; $22.50 for 18 holes & 1/2 cart, Wed–Fri
Carts: $8.50 / $17.00
Tee times: taken, not required; credit card guarantee for advance booking
Practice facilities: range & putting green
Clubhouse facilities: Cipriano's Restaurant; snack bar; banquet facilities
Outings: available for all sizes
League play: various times
Pro shop: well stocked
Lessons: by appointment; 3 teaching pros
Ranger: daily
Special rules: dress code